'This is a beautifully profound book
have to live many lifetimes to acquir
which intertwine so naturally anywa
the three questions asked of world renowned leaders and thinkers
about what advice they'd pass onto their grandchildren. Thoroughly
absorbing to read and life changing in its content. Definitely one to
pass to my children even before they have grandchildren!'

Rob Brown
Author of *'Build your reputation'* and CEO of The Networking Coaching Academy

'I was inspired by the authors and by the content. But, most of all, I
was inspired by the intent of this truly beautiful book!'

Derek Williams
Creator of *'The WOW! Awards'*, international speaker, and author of
'Wow! That's what I call service'

'A powerful masterpiece creating powerful generational bridges and
stories. Could easily rival some of the great management books of our
time. A far better book you are unlikely to find.'

Mark Lloydbottom
Author, international speaker and creator of IMPACT for Accountants

'Micro lessons in how YOU can expand the impact you have for good,
everyday. A must-read'

Martin Bissett
International keynote speaker and author of eight books, including
'Passport to partnership'

'A book that really does have the power to change millions of lives.
The world needs more books spreading messages like this.'

Andrew Griffiths
International bestselling author of 12 books, speaker and global mentor

'A truly inspiring insight into how you can make huge impacts in business, life and the world by doing extremely simple things. A must read.'

Phil Ellerby

Author of *'Do less work, earn more money'*, founder of Northern Accountants who are featured in the book *'The world's most inspiring accountants'*

'This book has incredible, life-changing wisdom that will positively impact every area of the reader's life. Jam-packed into the easy to read and navigate chapters is wisdom, learned over a lifetime, from 34 experts who have reached a high level of success, impact and influence in their industries. Well-worth the read.'

Tamika Hilder

Founder of *'Path of The Goddess'*, and one of the world's leading voices on personal development and consciousness - www.tamikahilder.com

'Paul Dunn and Masami Sato have created a movement of businesses that do well by doing good with B1G1. This book is a great example of "growing by giving". B1G1 gave each contributor the opportunity to give. Each writer now gives you their best advice. It's your turn to add your own and pass it on to your children and grandchildren.'

Roger James Hamilton

Founder of Entrepreneurs Institute, futurist, social entrepreneur and New York Times bestselling author

'We are often exposed to data, regularly bombarded with information, sometimes intrigued by knowledge and then - just occasionally - inspired by true wisdom. Now this inspiration can be a daily or even hourly occasion as a dip or deep dive into 'Better Business, Better Life, Better World' brings you ideas, thoughts and the much needed nudge to take action to change the world, your world, for the better and secure for yourself your rightful and valued place in the history of humankind. I love it. You will too...'

Peter Thomson

'The UK's most prolific information product creator' - www.peterthomson.com

'As a new Grandfather I can vouch for the wisdom that such a position brings. Cracking book with cracking ideas and a cracking purpose. Read it and take action to make the world a better place.'

Robert Craven

MD of The Directors Centre, speaker, author of books including *'The check-in strategy journal'*, *'Grow your digital agency'* and *'Bright marketing'*

'The B1G1 community is inspiring on every level - this book is another tangible reminder. A must read for any entrepreneur wanting to make a difference. Congratulations to all involved - and thank you for sharing your wisdom.'

Matthew Burgess

Director of View Legal, speaker, entrepreneur and author of *'The Dream Enabler'* series of books

'A goldmine of precious nuggets of wisdom, inspiration and opportunities for people wanting to make a difference. It is addictive and I felt compelled to keep reading in search of the next golden nugget which was never far away!'

Andy Gilbert

Author, facilitator, coach and developer of the Go M.A.D. (Making A Difference) Thinking System

'A great book for all of us with many wonderful thoughts and perspectives. I have already started quoting from it in my keynote presentations.'

Katie Kelly

Gold Medallist at the 2016 Rio Paralympics

'This is THE book to "win" the game of life! Everyone has their own definition of success but this book reaffirms that deep down we all just want to feel love, gratitude and have connections and experience these feelings with ourselves, with others and with causes bigger than ourselves. When we feel this way that's when the magic happens, that's when we are winning. If you follow the advice in this inspirational book you WILL have a better business, better life and live in a better world!'

Steven Briginshaw

Business mentor and author of the Amazon #1 bestseller *'The profits principles'*

Better business
Better life
Better world

Words of Inspiration to you today & always

Love Live Laugh & have fun

Joy & Love Helen & Guy

May 2017.

Edited by
Jonathan Pipe, Katie Pipe
and Laura Pipe

Copyright © 2016 Jonathan Pipe, Katie Pipe and Laura Pipe

First published 2016 by Gleneagles Publishing

This edition published 2016

A catalogue for this book is available from the British Library

All rights reserved. No part of this publication may be reproduced, stored in a retrieval system, or transmitted in any form or by any means, electronic or mechanical, photocopying, recording or otherwise without the prior written permission of the publishers.

Cover design by Steven Baldwin
Typeset by Steven Levers, Sheffield

First printed and bound in the UK

ISBN 978-1-5406-3831-1

This book is dedicated to our grandparents
and to grandparents and their grandchildren everywhere.

Contents

Chapter 1

Introduction

In June 2016 business leaders from across the world travelled to Bali.

Technically it was to attend a conference.

In reality, however, it was actually to celebrate the B1G1: Business For Good global movement. To cheer it on in its quest to make over 100 million meaningful micro impacts that would help to make businesses, lives and the world better (at the time of writing it has already achieved 90,594,955 impacts – and you can see the up to date total here www.b1g1.com).

Inspired by those numbers, the delegates said 'let's write a book together'.

And so this book was born.

About the authors

The 34 contributing authors were all delegates or keynote speakers at the conference in Bali. And they have all contributed their wisdom without payment.

They come from 4 continents, 7 countries, and collectively have written 38 other books. They are also all leading entrepreneurs, thinkers, researchers, practitioners or philanthropists, and include:

- Founders of major businesses and global charities
- Serial entrepreneurs and investors
- International keynote and motivational speakers
- Marketers and branding experts
- Consultants, coaches and trainers
- Leaders of internationally recognised professional service firms
- Ground-breaking doctors, dentists and psychologists
- An artist who has exhibited on four continents
- And they range in age from 13 to well past the point most people retire – and even include two young entrepreneurs who started a clothing business before they were teenagers, which has gone on to win international recognition.

Between them they have also:

- Advised governments
- Been involved in staging the Olympics
- Served customers ranging from one man band start-ups and not-for-profit organisations to Fortune 500 companies
- Won national and international awards and acclaim
- Launched game changing software companies
- Been featured by Forbes, Inc, The New York Times, The Huffington Post, CNN, The Telegraph, the BBC, on stage at TEDx and on many other leading media platforms.

The three questions behind the book

With that sort of pedigree and track record, their insights are clearly worth listening to.

But rather than minor insights, the book has been designed so that it only features their most profoundly important insights.

To achieve that, each author was asked to answer three (seemingly) simple questions:

1. If you could only pass on one piece of BUSINESS advice to your grandchildren, and you knew with absolute certainty that they would follow that advice throughout their time in business, what would that advice be?

2. If you could only pass on one piece of LIFE advice to your grandchildren, and you knew with absolute certainty that they would follow that advice throughout their lives, what would that advice be?

3. If you could only pass on one piece of advice to your grandchildren about MAKING THE WORLD A BETTER PLACE, and you knew with absolute certainty that they would follow that advice throughout their lives, what would that advice be? (NB: We told them that their answers here might relate to the environment, philanthropy, peace or anything else, and invited them to interpret and answer it as they wished).

By focusing them solely on the key advice they would give to their grandchildren, the book taps into the most powerful driver of human behaviour: the desire to see your descendants succeed.

As a result, the book contains:

- The most important lessons there are to learn – lessons that have taken 34 extraordinary people 34 lifetimes to learn

- The insights that will make things better for you, your family and everyone
- The shortcuts that make it easier - and the pitfalls to avoid.

The structure of each chapter

Most of the chapters are structured around those three questions: with the authors setting out their key advice to their grandchildren in a logical order under the headings 'Better business', 'Better life' and 'Better word'.

But for some of the authors it made more sense for them to arrange and present their advice in a different format. This, along with our 'light touch' editorial approach, means that the authentic voice of each of them shines through in their respective chapters.

The length of each chapter also varies, with some of the advice being direct and brief, and some of it being very detailed and comprehensive.

We believe this variety has resulted in an extremely readable, practical and useful book that you will want to refer back to many times over the months and years to come.

The big themes

It is impossible to produce a summary that does justice to the immense richness of insights in the chapters that follow. You have to read them yourself to understand their true power, be inspired, and get the full details you need in order to be able to use them to make things better in your business, your life and your world.

But in order to whet your appetite for the journey to come – both on these pages and beyond them – we do want to give you a flavour of some of the big themes. And we will also keep one of those themes as a secret bonus... at least until the end of this chapter, where it will provide the final piece of the jigsaw that makes everything else possible.

While some of the themes were perhaps to be expected, others are much more surprising. But they are all are equally profound.

Perhaps the biggest surprise, however, is the fact that many of these themes are the keys to making businesses AND life AND the world better. In other words, the solutions are interconnected rather than being isolated and independent of each other.

As a simple example, the act of smiling more can lead to a better customer service experience (BETTER BUSINESS), make you personally feel happier (BETTER LIFE) and brighten the day for all the people you smile at (BETTER WORLD). There are, of course, much more complex examples of this interconnectivity throughout the book. And your challenge is to identify and capitalise on them.

To help you, here is a brief and partial listing of 22 of the big themes in the advice the 34 authors would give to their grandchildren:

1. Work out what is important to you – your purpose, passion and priorities – and recognise that it may change over time

2. Follow your heart

3. Do what you love, and love what you do – that way it will never feel like work, you will become very good at it, and you will be very well rewarded financially and emotionally

4. If you don't love it, do something else – life is too short for anything else

5. Do something that really matters

6. Show your family that they really matter – be there for them, be with them and tell them that you love them

7. Recognise that each and every one of us really can make a difference

8. Connect and collaborate with inspiring and like-minded people – together you will make an even bigger difference

9. Understand that business can, and should, be a force for good

10. Build a business that solves meaningful problems

11. Understand what it does (and doesn't) mean to be a leader

12. Systemise your business – so that it doesn't depend on you, and can more easily grow, be replicated and make a difference to even more people

13. Ask great questions – because the quality of your life is shaped by the questions you ask

14. Listen – really listen

15. Do unto others as you would have them do unto you

16. Accept that mistakes and failures are good – as long as you learn from them

17. Make decisions – especially difficult decisions

18. Don't just talk, or even just make decisions – implement, take action, make things happen

19. Don't just be efficient (doing things well) - be effective (doing the right things well)

20. Contribute more than you consume – and give more than you take – freely, and without expectation of getting anything in return

21. Travel – it will open your eyes, bring you joy, and make you a better person

22. Understand that happiness is not about things, it is about feelings – so use less, waste less, live more and love more

If some of these themes sound simple, perhaps even simplistic, that is because no bullet points could ever convey the full richness, depth and detail of the insights the authors share in the rest of this book.

You have already seen the pedigree of the 34 authors. So you know that what they have to say – in its full richness, depth and detail - is categorically worth reading and reflecting on.

How to use this book

The chapters have been arranged in alphabetical order of author, so there is no need to start reading at the beginning and finish at the end.

You can do it that way if you want. But you can also simply dip in an out at random, jumping between chapters as they catch your eye.

Whichever way you approach it, we recommend that you:

- Read it all – there are so many powerful insights littered across the pages that you really can't afford to miss any of them
- Treat it as a work book rather than a library book – using a highlighter pen to identify the bits that resonate most with you, and annotate your thoughts in the margins
- Share the book with everyone in your business and family
- Take time to reflect on what you have read, and think about how you could apply this to your own business, your life and the world around you
- And use it all to create an action plan for your business, and for you personally

Your advice to your grandchildren

Of course, you also need to work out the advice you would give to your own grandchildren – and then make sure you follow it yourself.

To help you do precisely that, Appendix 5 has been created with practical guidance and lots of blank pages, so that you can:

- Become one of the authors by thinking through and writing down your advice to your grandchildren in the same format as the other authors
- Share your version of the book with your grandchildren, other loved ones, friends and anyone else you care about, and
- Ensure that you follow your own advice

A story in three parts

As our contribution, we would like to share a story from our lives.

Imagine the scene.

One day Ron was a strong and vibrant 64 year old. Quick to laugh. Even quicker to help. Everybody's friend.

The next day his life slipped away peacefully in his sleep. And seven painful days later, in front of 196 tearful mourners, his body slipped away too.

Surely nothing good could come out of that? That's what we thought at first. But how wrong we were.

The experience of Ron's death has helped us to learn three of the most important lessons life has to teach us.

Part 1 - A lesson in happiness

Throughout his life Ron worked hard. Very hard. In the eyes of others, perhaps even too hard.

But because he spent his life doing things he really loved, it never seemed like work to him. So he loved every minute. And he died a happy man.

If you were to die tomorrow, could people say the same about you?

And, if they couldn't, what are you going to do about it today, tomorrow and every day?

Remember, if you really want to do something you'll find a way - and if you don't, you'll find an excuse. So find a way to do more of the things you love - at home and at work. And enjoy every minute of every day as if it were your last.

Settling for anything less is a tragic waste.

Part 2 - A lesson in humility

Most people are lucky to get 30 or 40 people to their funerals. Ron had a staggering 196 - and very few of them were strictly family. In fact, it was standing room only at the church, and there were people on the street outside too. In addition, another 300 came to each of the two memorial concerts held in his honour a few weeks later.

Why was he so incredibly popular?

It wasn't because he was the life and soul of the party. Far from it. He was actually a slightly shy and very private man.

So what was his secret?

We think it was this... *he enjoyed his life best when he was helping others to enjoy theirs.*

It's as simple as that.

He was always first in line to help others. Through his work with countless community, church and charitable organisations he touched so many people's lives in a positive way. And in everything he did he really made a difference.

If you were to die tomorrow, could people say the same about you? And, if they couldn't, what are you going to do about it today, tomorrow and everyday?

Our point is not that we should all spend our lives doing more charity and community work - although the world would certainly be a better place if we did.

Instead our point is that the greatest rewards in life - both financial and emotional - go to those who make the biggest difference to the world around them.

Putting this into a business context for a minute, the moral is crystal clear. Bill Gates is one of the world's richest men because his software has made an enormous difference to the way the entire world works. And you too will be rewarded in business according to how much of a difference you make to the lives and businesses of your customers.

And because Bill became so successful, he has also been able to give back as a philanthropist... making a significant difference to the lives of millions of people via the Bill and Melinda Gates Foundation.

Part 3 – A lesson in how

Ron's story raises some big issues and questions. Perhaps even the biggest issues and questions any of us will ever face.

Ultimately, of course, it comes down to what we want out of life.

If, like us, you want to be happy, if you want to make a difference, and if you want to be fair to those you love, one thing is certain... it won't happen by chance.

You must make it happen.

So if you really want those things, start doing what you know you've got to do to get them. And start doing it today, because tomorrow could be too late.

The words 'if only I had' are the saddest in the English language.

Don't let them be yours.

A word about Ron

Actually, we are really proud to say that Ron was our Grandad. We are really proud of him. And we are really proud of the lessons he taught us.

Lessons that we know will also help you to build a better business. Lessons that will help you to create a better life for you and those you love. Lessons that will make the world a better, happier and more caring place.

Thanks Grandad.

... and a word from Ron's daughter

Ron's daughter – our Mum, Carol – was a delegate at the B1G1 conference in Bali. And afterwards she wrote this:

'I would love us all to live in a better and more peaceful world. At one level it sounds like an impossible dream. But actually it is much simpler than it sounds. What we need to do is to be involved, be connected, participate, and do whatever we can with joy in our hearts. As Mother Theresa said "Peace begins with a smile", and "we shall never know all the good that a simple smile can do". So let's start with the easy step of smiling more. After all, it is the small things that make the difference.'

The power of small

It really is the small things that make the difference.

In fact, the 'power of small' is probably the biggest and most frequently cited theme in the chapters that follow. It is also the 'bonus' theme we promised earlier.

The case for the power of small is overwhelming. For example, in the world of sport, the British cycling team was transformed from mediocrity to topping the medal table at three Olympic games in a row by making hundreds of very small changes (usually referred to as 'marginal gains'). Individually each of those gains was inconsequential. Collectively they were transformational.

The power of small both adds up and multiplies.

It adds up because, as one of our authors put it: 'If everybody alive today did one tiny thing every day to change our world, our world would change at a rate of 7.4 billion tiny things a day.'

And it multiplies because of the ripple effect – as one action informs, inspires or causes another, and another, and another.

None of us can do everything. But each of us can do something. And it is when we do that the magic happens.

And here's an example of that magic... just because you asked for a copy of this book, the life of at least one person in need somewhere in the world has been made a little bit better.

That difference has been funded by our authors, and delivered via www.b1g1.com.

So you have already made more of a difference than you realised.

Please read on to find out how you can do even more.

Chapter 2

Inspiration

This chapter contains a selection of inspiring quotes from the advice our authors would give to their grandchildren.

As you will see, however, we have deliberately chosen not to tell you where each of the quotes come from. Instead we hope that their anonymity will 'nudge' you into tracking them down by exploring the book in more detail.

Selected quotations

1. 'You have just one life, this life. Live it with passion and purpose, and take some time out every day to feel gratitude for all of the small wins along the way.'

2. 'Create and build businesses you love. Create and build businesses others love. Create and build businesses that are good for the world.'

3. 'Give regularly of your wisdom, time and whatever you can afford financially and be content with small yet regular progress. Real and meaningful change takes time and commitment.'

4. 'One trait that really sets successful entrepreneurs apart, is their bias towards implementation. They just get stuff done... and lots of it!'

5. 'If you know what's important, if it really matters to you and you have focus, you will find the time. If you don't find the time, it's because you either fail to understand the importance of the task, you lack focus or more likely, you are afraid.'

6. 'When you do good for someone, that act of kindness and generosity is generally either reciprocated, or, more importantly, replicated.'

7. 'Not all of us can do great things. But we can do small things with great love.'

8. 'The most comfortable seat doesn't always offer the best view.'

9. 'Step out of the fast lane and take the slow train from time to time.'

10. 'Being open to identifying our 'weaknesses' and accepting help is the formula that keeps a business achieving all that is possible.'

11. 'We distract ourselves by comparing ourselves to others. Instead look for your uniqueness. Magic always comes from uniqueness.'

12. 'Give of yourself without expectation and you will receive riches you cannot even imagine.'

13. 'Do what you love. Happiness, money and success will then follow you. The more you love what you do, and the more people it helps, the more successful you will be. The world will truly be a better place by you loving what you do.'

14. 'People are more alike than not alike. We want what is best for our families, friends and society at large. It is only when we are in a fearful or unhappy place that we don't want what is best for others.'

15. 'There are so many ways to give. To give a smile, a warm hand shake, hugs, a compliment. One of the most powerful gifts you can give, much more than money, is time. To be present with someone. In the moment. To listen and allow them to share with you a problem, a concern or an achievement. Even more importantly, they share their hopes and dreams with you.'

16. 'You cannot help everyone. But help who you can.'

17. 'Open your mind, seize opportunities to work, live, play, converse and share with as many different characters and cultures as you can.'

18. 'Every time you find yourself thinking about what you don't have, remind yourself that it is time to share what you do have.'

19. 'Life is a precious gift and can end at any time. People cling to it when it is almost gone, instead of making the most of it, in the fullness of every day.'

20. 'What is the Meaning of life? A life of Meaning. What is a life of Meaning? A life of Purpose. What is a life of Purpose? A life of Service.'

21. 'Effective communication begins with listening.'

22. 'If you sit at the bedside of a dying friend, rarely will you hear them express regret that they didn't buy that house on the water, drive that Ferrari, work longer hours or take the promotion. If there is regret, it will be about the amount of times they didn't say I love you to the people nearest, the hours they didn't come home early from work, the energy that went into the business or promotion and not into family, the inner journey that never received adequate attention, the time not spent with children, and so on. Meaning doesn't lie in things or material possessions – it lies within us and within our relationships!'

23. 'Find the difference you were born to make and give your whole heart into the service of that difference, so you can impact the greatest number of lives in the most sustainable way and leave your true legacy.'

24. 'Surround yourself with inspirational people who have new and different experiences to share with you. Learn from them and integrate into new circles.'

25. 'Be humble. But remember always that you are not inferior to, only less experienced than, the great leaders around you.'

26. 'Find a purpose, embrace inspiration, and most of all, believe in your ability to change the world.'

27. 'Pack a rucksack, grab your best friends, and travel as far as you can, experience as many things as possible and come home awakened, aware and ready to bring your experience to the table in your adult life.'

28. 'If everybody alive today did one tiny thing every day to change our world, our world would change at a rate of 7.4 billion tiny things a day.'

29. 'You don't have to figure it all out on your own. Connect with others and learn from people of all ages.'

30. 'You can do some amazing things on your own, and it's good to discover what you're capable of. It's even more incredible to build a team and create a bigger impact.'

31. 'Be focused on helping others as you go throughout your life. Don't leave it until you're older, more settled, more comfortable.'

32. 'Smiling is a language that everyone understands regardless of their past, their present or their future. Regardless of their age, their nationality, their situation or their state. It breeds positivity, confidence and love. It can be given and it can be received, anywhere and anytime, by and to anyone. It doesn't cost one cent. But it pays. And it keeps on paying for as long as it's remembered.'

33. 'Tell the people you love that you love them. Yes, my grandsons (and granddaughters), that means OUT LOUD, and at every opportunity.'

34. 'Never give up learning and improving on your knowledge. Education is the best investment that you can ever make.'

35. 'The journey of entrepreneurship is like being on a travelator that is going backwards... you have to keep moving and evolving or you will be left behind!'

36. 'Businesses have enormous potential to create great change in our world, far more than anything else can.'

37. 'Accept what has happened. What happened in the past cannot be changed no matter how hard you try. But the action you take now is totally under your control.'

38. 'You never know how many more days you have left to be here. So, do the best you can today.'

39. 'The present moment is the only thing that is ever real (and it's a gift; a real 'present' in every sense). Right now, you can only directly change the present moment, not your past and future. You are fully in control of how you feel, what you think and what you do right now at this present moment. It is the most powerful moment of your life.'

40. 'Don't be afraid to move on from your business when the passion for it starts to wane and you find yourself with a new interest.'

41. 'The good news is you don't have to solve all the world's problems - there are 7 billion of us, so if we all just pick one then we'd solve them all, so it doesn't matter which one you choose, just choose.'

42. 'Fame and fortune doesn't mean you're successful. Having a large bank balance and a flash car doesn't equate to success. Success isn't monetary. It is contentment and happiness in knowing you have done your best with what you have.'

43. 'Giving and getting both create happiness. Getting starts with what we don't have and isn't always in our control. Giving, on the other hand starts with what we already have and is always 100 percent in our control.'

44. 'We make a living by what we get, but we make a life by what we give',

45. 'Great businesses focus on simply enhancing the customer experience – creating or enhancing the value that their customers or consumers get out of life, in a way that is congruent with what the company does (its purpose)... creating value feels great, attracts great people and loyal customers - and is a sustainable way to be a part of something successful for the long term.'

46. 'There are only three truths in life. The first truth of life is that no one makes it out alive. The second truth of life is that they don't build hearses with luggage racks - you go out the way you came in and take nothing with you. The third truth of life is it will be exactly what you make it.'

47. 'It is up to you what you believe in. It is for no one else to say what has to be important to you. Whatever you choose, choose it because it is something you believe in and are passionate about - not because other people are passionate about it.'

48. 'The way to make a difference is to simply go first.'

49. 'For every decision you need to make, look at your business through your customer's eyes.'

50. 'A better world comes from when we add significantly more positive value than you or your decisions consume. This doesn't mean a balance favouring your good deeds over your wicked ones. It means contributing more to this world than the world gifts you.'

51. 'Travel will also give you a much better appreciation of the world, and your place it in. It will help you understand how lucky you are. And it will help you to see what you can do to help those who are less lucky.'

52. 'Earn with love, pay with love.'

53. 'Your family will not always be with you. So cherish the time you have together. Make the very most of it. And do it now, because you never know what tomorrow will bring.'

54. 'The best way to live your life is to appreciate what you've got, be with the ones you love, and share your love with your family, your community and the world.'

55. 'Write down everything you do and exactly how you do it in the form of a set of detailed step by step instructions. These instructions then become the systems on which your business is based.'

56. 'Use your heart as your compass.'

57. 'Invest more of your time and yourself into finding and nurturing the great relationships of your life.'

58. 'Everyone that I know who has retired seems to live a shorter life. So keep working - be it voluntary work or in advisory roles. And when you do, you will be more valuable than ever, because age gives you life experiences that cannot be taught.'

59. 'Reduce your digital intake of information and increase your communication with others. The world is full of stimulating people when you give yourself a digital detox.'

60. 'The more you give, the more you will receive. The more you receive, the more you have to share.'

61. 'There's a way for people to simultaneously derive a personal sense of meaning, improve the global economy and repair our habitat in time for us to survive.'

Grandparent's advice

Celebrate the little wins

Based in Australia, Adam is:

- An international keynote speaker specialising in social media for business
- One of Australia's leading experts in harnessing the power of LinkedIn for business
- Consultant to private clients in Australia, New Zealand, North America, The Middle East and Singapore
- Over 5,200 people globally have sought his skill and insights to leverage the power of LinkedIn
- Author of two books, 'Social media secret sauce' and 'The LinkedIn playbook'
- A featured columnist for MOB Magazine, an Australian national business publication

Here is the advice he would give to his grandchildren...

Better business

Before you even start your business work from your end game back to your starting point. Business plans are fine, but knowing where you want to end up before you start will give you a clear path to success. Taking the time to create your roadmap at the beginning will make it easier to employ aligned team members who understand why you are in business and your purpose.

Stay true to your purpose, it will always guide you through the good times and the bad that is the business journey. You can count on plenty of both occurring no matter what stage of the business lifecycle you are on.

When your team understand and are aligned with that purpose they will be your greatest allies through the tough times. Make sure you tell them often how important they are to you and the business success and never refer to them as 'employees', it is the most disempowering word you can even use. They are your team. Lead by example on purpose, and they will walk through hell by your side every step of the way.

Should you ever need funding from investors or financial institutions, being able to clearly outline where you sit at that point, where you started and where you are heading will be crucial in winning their support. Being able to show you have a team that support you and are all superstars in their own right will open those doors. Your purpose and your story will be every bit as important as your Profit and Loss or Balance Sheet.

Celebrate the little wins as often as possible, the big wins are always a series of little ones strung together.

> 'It is not enough that we do our best, sometimes we must do what is required.'
> Winston Churchill

Better life

You have just one life, this life. Live it with passion and purpose, and take some time out every day to feel gratitude for all of the small wins along the way.

Travel the world and experience all that it has to offer. Experiencing the many diverse cultures around the world will open your eyes to just how amazing this planet is and that there is good and bad in every culture or society - ours included.

Make a commitment to yourself to travel overseas at least once every year, lock the date into your calendar at least six months in advance. Spend a little time every week leading up to your departure date learning something new about the people and the things you will do when you arrive to experience as much as you can while you are there.

Terrorism across the globe is a real and ugly truth. Don't let it stop you experiencing all of the wonderful places there are to see and immerse yourself in. But do, of course, be sensible and aware of current threats.

> 'He who is not courageous enough to take risks will accomplish nothing in life.'
> Muhammad Ali

Better world

Find a group of like-minded individuals doing great things to make our world a better place. For together you will stay focused on your cause and accountable to each other.

Give regularly of your wisdom, time and whatever you can afford financially and be content with small yet regular progress. Real and meaningful change takes time and commitment.

Embed whatever social good you choose to stand for into your everyday business actions. This way you will be practicing what you preach and your reputation for being a leader in your chosen field and a leader for change will be established.

Once you become known for these beliefs and actions, others will seek to join you in changing the world one small step at a time. As more people believe in your cause, and see you leading by example, your movement for change will gain momentum. And as that momentum grows the proof of your small yet consistent actions will be obvious in the improved lives or cleaner environment you have created.

The satisfaction in knowing you played some part in creating this change will be one of the most rewarding highlights of your life.

'How wonderful it is that nobody need wait a single moment before starting to improve the world.'
Anne Frank

Be open to growth, experiences and responsibilities

Based in Australia, Alfio is:

- An 'Accountant For Good' and an advisor that works with business owners seeking to improve their business and in turn their lives
- He believes that one of the fastest ways to do this is to help business owners work on Leadership – first their own leadership, and then the leadership in their business

Here is the advice he would give to his grandchildren...

Better business

Business: 'a person, partnership, or corporation engaged in commerce, manufacturing, or a service; profit seeking enterprise or concern'. That is a definition of a business. At the core of every business is a person, or persons.

The advice that I offer, which has served me well, is: 'Your Business will never out grow You'

When I first heard this it was as confronting then as it is today. We like to believe that things happen outside of ourselves, however I believe that we are at the centre of our lives and of all that we do, and this is especially evident in business.

If a business is successful, examine the people and the leaders in that business and you will find that these people are constantly growing themselves. So it's no surprise that their business grows with them.

When a business is not performing, a financial analysis can give indicators of where improvement can be made. However, you will not have to look too far from the Leaders in these businesses to get a great insight into why the business is not performing to its full potential.

The advice 'Your Business will never outgrow You', asks you to know yourself. The advice challenges you: Do you know what your strengths are? Are you working to improve on these strengths? Or do you believe that you are beyond improving?

The advice equally asks you to know your weaknesses. Are you willing to admit to them? Are you willing to address them?

I have found that the sooner you realise that you do not know everything, and learn to question all things and seek support from those qualified to give you the right support, then you start to grow.

The magic then is that, as you grow, everything around you is able to grow with you, especially your business.

Your Business will never outgrow You.

Better life

Life is everything. We are born. We will die. And in-between is life. It has been said that the only constant in life is change, so learn to accept this and be willing to adapt to change.

Ultimately life is meant to be enjoyed and experienced.

And often this will be in the most pleasant of ways. These can be celebrations of achievements like the birth of children and grandchildren. Or the passing of milestones in birthdays and festive occasions shared with family, friends and new acquaintances. And all the time we are experiencing life as it unfolds.

Other times we experience life through pain. At first this pain is such that we seek to run away from it as far and as quickly as we can. But in time we come to understand that there is a lot of value in the lessons that painful experiences give us if we are willing to ask 'what have I learnt from this'?

Life for me has been about experience. So my advice is to seek out as many experiences as you can. As time goes by it will be these experiences that will add so much value to your life and, in turn, to the lives that you will come into contact with.

Sometimes you won't understand the value of the experience immediately, however it will enrich your life and the day will come when you share the value of your experience.

Life - experience it.

Better world

We do not exist in isolation, and no one does anything great alone. So making the world a better place is a responsibility that befalls all of us.

This responsibility is perplexing, because it would appear that fulfilling it is voluntary, either consciously or subconsciously.

We can all agree and subscribe to the notion that we should make the world a better place. For many however that's where it stops. Making the world a better place suddenly becomes someone else's responsibility. Sadly that's how I lived a large part of my life.

Fortuitously I have had the good fortune to come across some remarkable mentors and family members who have opened up my life and reality to what making the world a better place can mean for me, and the world.

Making the world a better place requires me to be a part of that world, so the question for me became am I making myself a better person? Am I developing, growing and thinking outside of myself? Am I able to buy in into a bigger vision or willing to play a bigger game?

So the advice is, accept first that you want to make the world a better place. Then set about becoming a better you, and start impacting those around you in a positive way.

Immediately you will start to make the world a better place!

Surround yourself with kindness and support

Based in the UK, Aynsley:

- Is the CEO of Tayabali Tomlin, a multi-award winning firm of accountants based in Cheltenham
- Works with owner-managed businesses throughout the UK to help them grow and scale sustainably, increase profits, reduce tax bills and plan for exit
- Was ranked number 4 in #Economia50 – a list of the most influential sources of finance news and information in the UK on social media during 2015
- Is an advisory board member of the B1G1 worthy cause partner Free to Shine based in Siem Reap, Cambodia and has participated in a number of study tours to see B1G1 worthy cause partners in Cambodia and India

Here is the advice he would give to his grandchildren...

Better business

We all know of, or have seen, people paralysed by fear. In fact, we see it regularly in life, on television programmes, at sporting events or in the cinema. In our personal life, we are often afraid of new or different activities or challenges. For many, being asked to stand up in front of a crowd of 400 at a business conference and give an impromptu speech, sing or perform a modern dance interpretation would bring them out in a cold sweat! The fear of the unknown can be so great, that we find excuses to hide, delay or ultimately wriggle out of undertaking the task. The same applies in business too.

I have advised hundreds of business owners over the past fifteen years, and those that succeed tend to have a number of common characteristics, such as drive, ambition, talent etc. However, the one trait that really sets those successful entrepreneurs apart, is their bias towards implementation. They just get stuff done... and lots of it!

Failure To Implement or 'FTI' is one of the biggest barriers to success in business. Most people assume that FTI is down to the fact that business owners don't know what to do, they don't have the skill set, it's too difficult or they are looking for perfection before taking action.

However, one of the most common excuses I hear from business owners is; 'I just don't have the time'. In fact, because it is such a common excuse, there have been many books and courses written on time management.

Whilst I agree that time management is an important skill to add to your arsenal, if you know what's important, if it really matters to you and you have focus, you will find the time. I really believe that if you don't find the time, it's because you either fail to understand the importance of the task, you lack focus or more likely, you are afraid.

I prefer to think of FTI as Fears Tempt Inaction.

Fear, I believe, comes from three main sources:

1. Fear of failure,
2. Fear of the unknown, and
3. Fear of ridicule

To combat fear of failure, we can analyse the risks, plan a course of action, look to what others have done in the past, set targets and create stepping-stones along the way. But ultimately, it is important to take action - to just do it! We can and should, of course, also regularly monitor performance against targets, review progress regularly and change our plans and actions when necessary. To do otherwise would be reckless.

Fear of the unknown and fear of ridicule can in many ways be harder to overcome. I know that when I step outside my comfort zone, two things happen. My comfort zone gets bigger and magic happens. You have got to trust and believe in yourself. What is the worst that could happen? I know from experience, the rush, excitement and satisfaction I feel when I've accomplished a task or undertaken an activity that I've never done before. As Nike says, 'Just do it'. And remember, the power of any idea is only ever in its implementation.

I think it's important to remember that we all really want to see people succeed deep down. And, we feel for and empathise with those who are doing something new or different, those that are facing a challenge. We root for them. If people are not rooting for you, if they are ridiculing you, then they are not truly good friends, colleagues or team members and you need to say goodbye to them.

Better life

Ultimately you have the choice of whom you choose to hang around with.

You can choose to surround yourself with positive, happy, enthusiastic, supportive people and those that are looking to make a difference to themselves, those around them and the wider world. Or, you can choose to surround yourself with negative, aggressive, angry people - people who constantly gossip or never have a kind word to say about anything or anybody.

Who would you choose?

Some of my friends believe that, either because of peer pressure or friendship, they have to go along with the beliefs, ideas and actions of their so-called friends or those with whom they are associated. You really don't have to, and shouldn't continue friendship or association with those who make you feel unhappy or bad.

It's also important to appreciate that, rightly or wrongly, you are judged by the company you keep and the actions and behaviours of those who are within your group or network.

Of course, we all have bad days – days when we are down or negative - but this is when true friends raise us up, not drag us down even further. We also sometimes look at things from the wrong perspective. That's when great friends are able to give us a view from a position where we are not.

You need to find and surround yourself with those people who share your values and beliefs. Those that are aligned with and inspire you. At the firm where I work, we have spent a lot of time creating a culture built around ten core values. We protect ruthlessly and maintain that culture and those values by only choosing to work with people who believe in the culture and share the values.

You need to find friends and colleagues that challenge you to be the best you can be, and who show you and others around you kindness and generosity of actions and spirit.

Better world

Changing the world is a huge ask for any one person. However, if all of us play a little part, bit by bit, together we can move mountains.

It's the power of small.

Isn't it also interesting that, when you do good for someone, that act of kindness and generosity is generally either reciprocated, or, more importantly, replicated. Whether you are religious or not, everyone has heard the phrase '*do unto others as you would have them do unto you*', which is a fantastic life philosophy whichever way you look at it.

And whilst we know this to be true of friends, not many of us have experienced this with strangers. A brilliant example of the reciprocity of kindness is a story I heard from the CEO, Nicky Mih, of Free to Shine, a Non Governmental Organisation (NGO) that I'm extremely proud to be a part of. Free to Shine operates in Siem Reap, Cambodia and identifies girls at risk of sex trafficking and empowers them with an education to prevent sex slavery.

Nicky told me the story of Chovvy, who had been on the programme for a year and a half: 'She is 14 and has five younger brothers and sisters. One year ago her father died in a tragic road accident, placing her, as the eldest daughter, at even greater risk of leaving school to support her family. We provided a little additional help to this family while they were in crisis. Not only has Chovvy stayed in school, but she asked our team for a whiteboard and a marker so that she could start teaching younger children Khmer Literacy and basic English. Of course we said yes, and Chovvy has set up evening classes and already has 10 students! A remarkable young girl. More and more of our girls are helping each other with their homework, sharing their library books with their siblings and grandparents and even holding their own classes, showing us just how important education is, and their inherent desire to share their skills and knowledge'.

This is a beautiful act of kindness and demonstration of the philosophy '*do unto others as you would have them do unto you*'.

'No act of kindness, however small, is ever wasted'
Aseop

We all want to live in a better world and we all want to play a part in making that happen. By showing others kindness and generosity, we know that they will do the same - creating a massive ripple effect!

Become a key person of influence

Based in Australia, Benjamin is:

- A young entrepreneur with over 13 years' experience developing indoor Family Entertainment Centres.
- Creative Director and founder of Laserzone, an indoor Laser Tag brand with five locations around Australia
- Consultant to the Laser Tag industry, helping clients improve the performance of their facilities
- Australasia's highest ranked Laser Sporting player and the most decorated Laser Sporting player in Australasian history
- Member of the world's number two ranked Laser Sporting team, the QLD Maroons
- Laser Tag Australasian Championships and World Championships Council member

Here is the advice he would give to his grandchildren...

Better business

It is commonly accepted that the recipe for success in business is determined by a whole range of factors. And those factors can be vastly different depending on the industry, geographical location, time and stage of maturation of the organisation.

There are certainly stories of people or organisations, 'tripping across' the right business formula at the right time, in the right industry. However, on the whole, business success is most commonly a deliberate act. A sequence of good decisions and actions that lead to the achievement of the goals that a person or organisation has set out to achieve.

So if it is our goal to be part of a successful organisation, then the question is how do we find these 'good decisions' and take 'good actions'? Where do we start? How do we even know what questions we should be asking?

Following on from Simon Sinek's ground-breaking 2011book 'Start with why', there is a commonly held belief that intention is a key part of the business success model. By being super clear on our intent, and demonstrating this to the outside world through our actions, we can inspire people to come along for the ride, purchasing our product or possibly even joining our team.

Simon's key phrase was, 'people don't buy what you do, they buy why you're doing it'. And indeed there are many examples of this in action.

Apple sells many more computer and mobile telephone products than their competitors who (arguably) boast better technology. For many users, having an Apple product is not about the technology – it is more about the trust Apple have built over many years of selling sleek, beautiful, well designed products.

On the flip side, there are countless stories of organisations with great intentions that fail due to circumstances that range from poor cash management to a lack of business strategy or diversification.

One could even argue that there are many successful organisations that do not have good intentions. Whether these organisations can survive in this changing business landscape is another discussion.

However, the question remains, if we were to refine our understandings of the business world into tenets that stand the test of time, what philosophies can we carry forward confidently, knowing that they will apply in 5, 10 or 100 years' time? We know that there are important factors such as intent, or having a good product. But we are looking for more than this. We are looking for universal principles. Principles that are fundamental to all successful organisations, and will stand up in the face of factors that could change at any stage of the business life cycle.

In a stand-out book from Jim Collins in 2001 called 'Good to Great', a comprehensive study was conducted looking only at the very top performing companies over a 40 year period to see how they did it. It searched for the common parameters that influenced the best performing organisations.

When I read it back in 2009, it completely changed my view of how organisations work. It demonstrated to me that there were, in fact, key principles that we can rely upon, even in a rapidly changing business environment.

And the biggest relief for me was that it didn't require me to have all the answers!

Jim and his team highlighted a series of key factors for organisational success. However, I think the most profound insight from this book is that we must, 'get the right people on the bus, and in the right seats'. Put first things first, and figure out who the right mix of people are for the organisation before determining the business strategy.

This philosophy flies in the face of how the vast majority of organisations are now run.

In most cases, the leader usually determines a business strategy they would like to implement, and then goes looking for people to help them execute a pre-existing strategy.

But, in fact, the most successful organisations do it the other way around. They first find good people. People that are aligned with the intent that is being held in the heart and mind of the creator or chief executive of the organisation. Once the right mix of people have come together and are clear on the roles that they play, then a business strategy can be created that utilises the collective experience and wisdom of the key people.

By identifying and attracting the right people to the organisation, good decisions and positive actions become a natural result, instead of a continual struggle. And the right people, with the right level of autonomy to make decisions in the right area of the organisation, will naturally create patterns of good decisions.

If good decisions are being made and good actions are being taken, then the organisation will habitually have the right products and services at the right times, in the right markets with the right marketing and business strategy.

The right people will know when to diversify, when to simplify, when to research, when to expand, when to shrink, when to employ, when to change and when to stay put and consolidate.

So, if I was to offer one piece of universal business advice for my grandchildren, it would be that it is all about people. And therefore you should focus on really understanding people and the art and science of human connectivity, human nature and human profiling systems.

I also suggest that you learn how to become a key person of influence, so that having all the answers becomes an obsolete quest. Because the ability to influence key people towards a philosophy, an idea or an organisation is a fundamental ingredient for business success.

Better life

Growing up as a regular suburban boy, it was clear to me that something wasn't quite right with the way people were encouraged to behave and plan their lives in the modern world. It appeared so odd to me that people would work in the same occupation for so many years, happy to leave the big questions locked away in the attic.

Questions such as 'is this really making me happy?', or 'is this the best use of my unique skills and talents?'

It seemed that people felt content to make the same decisions as everyone else.

In no particular order, the general process involved doing as well as you could at school or in a trade. Build a career. Find a partner. Get married. Buy a house. Have children. Spend the rest of your life shopping and working, with the occasional trademark family holiday. All of this was done with an eye on the future. Maybe one day, you could relax and enjoy the last few years of existence as a retiree, and perhaps have enough superannuation accumulated to live a moderate existence.

For me, all of this felt painful to even think about.

If the thought of having to choose one profession wasn't enough to send me in to an anxiety attack, the thought of being tied down to one house or one partner felt like a planned imprisonment. All I could think to myself was, 'what if I don't like my house or partner anymore?' And 'what if I want to change?'

As I matured, I realised that there was absolutely nothing wrong with any of these life decisions, as long as we have a free will choice – ie the ability to discern for ourselves what our life is going to look like. And in fact, I realised that I was incredibly lucky to be born into a privileged society where we are able to make these decisions for ourselves.

Having this realisation led to a new and perhaps even more perplexing question. If we have the ability to make any choice we want, why do we seem to see so many people making the same choices that do not lead them to their ultimate happiness?

With all the accumulated wisdom on our planet, surely we would have mastered the art of happiness by now.

It truly boggled my mind that people would stay in jobs that they did not like, or stay with partners that did not make them happy, or make life decisions that just didn't seem like they were heading towards their ultimate happiness. And it wasn't until it came time for me to choose what I wanted to do after High School that I began to understand why these patterns are so prevalent in our society.

As a 17-year-old, I had absolutely no idea what I wanted to do for a career. So much so, that I chose to do a Commerce degree because it was open ended enough that I wouldn't really need to decide what occupation I would end up in for a long time.

When I made this decision, Commerce was definitely not my passion, and in fact, all I thought about at the time was when I was going to be able to jump back on my guitar and learn that new Metallica solo. But there was no way, I was going to pursue a music career. There were simply not enough jobs around to guarantee my success. And in addition to that, my parents would definitely have been disappointed with such a career choice.

It was at this point I began to see why we seem to make choices that lead us away from our ultimate happiness.

I saw that it is the expectations of our image makers such as our parents, our governments and our friends that have a really significant impact on our decision making. And I look back now and wonder what choices I would have made, had I not been influenced by the expectations of those around me.

The years that followed were some of the most difficult years of my life.

At the age of 22 I had, what felt like at the time, a mid-life crisis that came around 20 years too early. I choreographed my energy entirely around what my mind thought was the best for the future. Work really hard, do everything myself and fill every spare minute with study so that I can get the best grades possible and set myself up for the future. If I am really lucky, I might even be able to become a merchant banker in Hong Kong and have a 6-digit salary in my first few years out of university!

I can now see that I was deeply disconnected from my own authority, and from my own natural flow. My whole perspective was based on false ideas around money equalling happiness, and that working really hard was the pathway to success in my career.

By the time I finished university, I was so burnt out, that I completely swung in the opposite direction. I became lazy and uninspired by my work. I began to smoke a lot of pot to help me relax, and I began doing less of the things that I used to love such as playing guitar and body boarding. The imbalance in my life had led to a series of toxic patterns that took me years to unravel.

I now look back and realise that this is all part of my story. All of these things have shaped me in to the person I am now. I still work hard, but I do it more consciously than before. I work with a better understanding of why I am doing what I am doing, and how much rest and play are required to maintain balance. All of these experiences have shaped what is potentially, one of my most precious personal values.

If I could share only one piece of advice about life with my grandchildren it would most definitely be...

'Follow your own authority'

There is a wisdom inside of us, that does not come from the mind, that hooks us into our natural trajectory of life. Simply put, it is our own inner authority. It knows what's best for us, and guides us to make consistently good decisions in alignment with our greatest good.

This does not mean that life becomes easy. For example, if it is our goal to be 'a great business leader', then life is going to offer us opportunities to become a great business leader. These opportunities are typically disguised as challenges and difficulties – and will help us ascend to a new level of self, so that we can become that which we desire. The correct goal therefore, is not to eliminate challenges, but to reach new levels of consciousness and response in the face of these challenges.

The more we listen to our own inner authority, and the less we listen to our conditioned beliefs and the expectations of our own image makers, the more we slip in to the natural trajectory of our life.

The resistance in life begins to slip away. Life becomes more of a dance and a flow, rather than a struggle, and we accelerate our pathway to our ultimate goals.

Better world

For many of us, making the world a better place means doing something big and drastic to prove our devotion to the planet. We need to go off the grid. We need to stop burning fossil fuels. We need to chain ourselves to a tree.

But for most people, these things are impractical and are not a realistic way to impact the world in a positive way.

A very wise woman by the name of Mother Teresa once said, 'Not all of us can do great things. But we can do small things with great love'.

When I first heard this quote, it warmed my heart.

It encompasses so much hope for all of us. Indeed, if everyone from the street sweeper to the rocket scientist approached our worldly activities with great love and care, our mindfulness around our interactions in the world would be completely transformed.

Every interaction would inspire us to take our shining out into the world, and give us the energy we need to push through the difficulties that we face in everyday life.
What's more, this is a realistic goal. It's a simple decision by each of us to take love and care into our work. Love and care for the work, the world, ourselves and others.

So if I was to offer my grandchildren one piece of advice that could help make the world a better place, it would be to bring their shining in to every part of their life.

It does not matter what you do, what is important is how you do it.

If it is your intent to become a janitor at the local mall, then clean those toilets like you really care for the sanitation of the people who will be using them. If you want to be a cab driver, then take care to make each and every guest feel welcome, and happy that they jumped in the car with you.

It is in this way that we demonstrate to each other what it is to be human, and bring out the best of what each and every person has to offer.

The great work of art

Based in Singapore, Booth is:

- Author of 'Significance, How to Align Money and Meaning in the Well Lived Life'
- Co-founder of World Wings Day [Nov 19th] - Putting Wings on Your Vision
- Enables successful, time starved leaders to express the opulence of their human spirit through the 5 step ARTS™ process
- A successful conceptual artist exhibited in the USA, Spain, Germany, Australia and at the Museum of Art and Design in Singapore
- In her alter ego, Joanne Flinn, she is a former banker and technologist, and co-founded The Change Leaders, a professional practice group from the University of Oxford and HÈC Paris that focuses on the human side of change

Here is the advice she would give to her grandchildren...

Better business

A great business is a great work of art. Great works of art expand our vision of what is possible. The most powerful way to do this is to see your business as an extension of you and your purpose for being here. Purpose with presence is powerful.

Business, in whichever form you do it, is your way of showing up and contributing to the world. It's less about 'Is it for profit or not?' or the legal form of a private limited company or NGO. Instead, it is more about the values you hold and choose to live through your business.

Your values form the colours, forms, textures, hues, sound, scents, materials and processes used to create your business. They are what inspires you, what gives you meaning and what attracts others to you as customers, partners and staff.

How does this look in practice? As an artist, I explore how we can expand ourselves and our souls as humans, while making this planet a better place. So these same values show up in the technologies and the materials used in creating my art with meditation, conservation and wonder. Equally importantly, business is a team creation, and my patrons, clients and partners share these values.

What are your values?

In business, begin with being present to the values you truly wish to live by and be.

What is being present? Presence is being fully here, right now.

In business, being present is the most powerful place to be. You feel what is really going on with those who are part of your business eco-system — your customers, staff, shareholders, regulators and the public.

What does this take?

Drop the worry about the future, and simply focus on this moment with them and ask 'Tell me more?' with genuine curiosity, and then listen. Ask again and listen. Ask again and listen. Be listening. Problems will simplify and dissolve. Wisdom and wealth will come.

Then from listening, into presence in action.

Values drive actions. Notice what your values are in the moment by the choices you make. Watch yourself as you go about your day, as you make decisions in your business, as you prioritize efforts and passion, as you focus energy and funds.

Values-in-action are the values that show up in your actions and choices. These are what create power and presence.

For example, take these two contrasting values - distrust and trust. Something happens. The actions one takes differ based on values:

- If someone acts from distrust, they will see things that don't work out the way they want - a problem and evidence of bad intention on the other party. The relationship or agreement tends to sour.

- What happens if you operate from trust? When something unexpected happens with a business partner, you'll be more likely to enquire, seek to understand and find a solution that works for both of you.

Successful businesses, like many things in life, are an accumulation of many small decisions, actions and moments that all align.

Stuff happens, but your values in action are your choice.

Better life

Live. Be present in who you are in the world. Come from your heart.

It's easy to be well educated and use our minds like the fabled rapier swords of old, or like a modern surgical weapon or laser. Life lived from the mind dries out. The sap and energy that gives joy, passion and meaning comes from the heart.

Life is a great artwork. Life created from a mind may be well executed. It might be technically good. But if it does not touch the soul, then it's not great art. When your life touches your soul, and even the souls of others, you'll feel a vibrancy, the zing of living with your heart alive.

Yes, life may do things, stuff happens, but it's your heart to open or close. And it is up to you how you choose to respond. Is it to worry, fear the future, regret the past or simply to acknowledge 'OK, this happened'?

Fear makes sense if we have a sabre tooth tiger coming towards us. Or a speeding car. But at this precise moment, neither is likely to be true. Fear is a mind game to stop playing. Likewise, regrets and might-have-beens are useful as an indicator for wiser choices, but not as definition of who you are.

Living from the heart is a positive choice that gives infinite possibilities. It opens up the sense that the heart connects, that love is a space of understanding, that life is abundant and much is possible.

It's a very different choice to living from fear, disconnection, distrust, limitation and lack of opportunity.

See your mind as a wonderful tool that you can use to create amazing things... and power this vision from the heart. Life flows from this space. It's a wondrous place of adventure and exploration.

Yes things happen. What would skiing or surfing be if there wasn't the variation, the thrills and the spills? The initial trying, the falls, the learning to balance, the trying of something new, even more difficult. It's experimenting (the positive word for failure). And experimenting is what helps our lives grow and us to develop.

When our hearts are open to experimentation, new things are possible.

Hearts put lift into the wings of our visions in life.

The first time you tried to walk or use a pencil was messy, but your heart encouraged you. Now, you are a master with both. Stuff that happens simply gives you space to try something new and open your heart.

Live your life as the great artist. Great art is created from the heart.

Better world

As you live life, give to the world.

Choose your vision of what you wish the world to be. Your vision can be as big or small as you wish.

Then, give what you wish to see around you, what you wish to experience. The world is really the biggest part of us, so as you give to the world, you are also strangely giving to yourself, as you too are part of the world.

For example, if you wish to see wealth, give wealth and help. If you wish for health, give health and kindness. If you wish for love, give love and companionship. A wise man once told me, 'If I want watermelons, I plant watermelon seeds. Planting oranges wouldn't get me melons'.

This is a nourishing way of living in a busy world. Gandhi called it being the change you wish to see.

It's being present, acting on your values. This is being. Giving forward as you wish the world to be is like planting seeds... and seeds grow.

And they show up in your world and in the world around you.

By being deliberate and giving what you wish to experience, you'll focus on what you wish for, not for what you don't wish for. When giving it to others, observe and make sure it's something they truly wish for (be present, connect from the heart). And once you have, celebrate that you have contributed to the good in the world.

If you've counted, you'll have done four good things... the thought/ intention, the planning and alignment to their wishes, the doing of it and the celebration of doing good.

And those four things add up - sometimes fast like a river, sometimes minutely - like drips of water gradually changing a rock.

Time flows easily when your business in life comes from your values, when it's life lived from your heart and you are giving forward to others.

May each day of your life be your gift to the world and a great work of art.

Travel, travel and then travel some more

Based in Bali where he lives with his wife Tet and son Sam, Chris is:

- CEO and Founder of Mass Participation Asia – an annual industry conference
- Author of the book 'Mass Participation Sporting Events' published in December 2015
- Founder and former CEO of Spectrum Worldwide (SWW) – where he was involved in organising events for over one million people during a 25 year period, including the Sydney 2000 Olympics, some of Asia's biggest events and a multitude of charity events. SWW was sold to IRONMAN in 2016
- A consultant to brands, governments and events
- A sought after speaker, entrepreneur and creator of intellectual property

Here is the advice he would give to his grandchildren...

Better business, better life, better world

For as long as I can remember travel has been a part of my life - and probably one of my biggest sources of education and inspiration. It started in Zimbabwe where I grew up poor on a farm and, at last count, I have been lucky enough to have visited 43 countries and many of the world's most iconic destinations.

In the early days it was travelling around my country, more often than not as a hitch-hiker during school holidays, or on camping trips with my family. I have stayed in amazing five star hotels and stunning beach resorts, and worked on multi-million-dollar charter boats in the Mediterranean. But it is not all about money and luxury.

For me it's about the amazing people I have met, the many cultures I have been part of, the beautiful scenery I have experienced, and the multitude of life lessons. Indeed, many of the best experiences have been on a shoestring budget with a pack on my back.

So here I will share three of my many experiences, and explain their relevance to helping you experience, enjoy and create a better life, better business and better world.

Travelling in New Orleans, USA

'Give it up, I've got a gun'...

... said the voice from behind me as I walked along the New Orleans sidewalk in the dark of night. I instantly let go of my small backpack, only to turn around and see my girlfriend being dragged along the footpath, hanging on to her handbag for dear life.

'Let go, let go' I screamed.

What unfolded over the next half hour was like a scene from a movie. After checking that my girlfriend was OK, I flagged down the first passing car. The driver, a plain clothes policeman, reached down, put a blue flashing light on his dashboard and told us to get in. We raced off down the street to see if we could find the attackers - to no avail.

Within minutes of returning to the scene of the holdup three police cars, sirens blazing, screeched to a halt. The first policeman to get out greeted us in a gruff voice 'what the F... are you doing here, you're lucky you weren't killed.'

Seconds later a white pickup screeched to a halt and a man jumped out, holding my girlfriend's handbag and shouting 'I got de purse, I got de purse'. He had seen us being mugged and had chased after the muggers - who then dropped the bag in fear and escaped as he almost ran them down.

With a police escort we then went back to the dark side street where he had found the handbag. There we found my backpack, our passports lying separately on the road and all of our belongings.

Total damage done: one pair of broken sunglasses and a scratch on my girlfriend's back where she had been dragged.

A very lucky escape.

The man who had come to our rescue then invited us to collect our campervan from the supposedly safe campsite down the road and come to park in his front yard. He was not a wealthy man, but lavished hospitality and many simple gifts on us for the next two days to ensure that we experienced some 'great southern hospitality' to compensate for our not so hospitable experience.

Travelling in Sri Lanka

The whistle blew as the packed train trundled out of the station in Galle in the south of Sri Lanka.

Despite the close attentions of a tout who assured us of a seat when we arrived at the station, our 'seat' ended up being sitting on the floor of the carriage with our feet dangling outside over the steps.

We were heading to Kandy for the world famous Perahera - a stunning street festival with thousands of drummers, dancers, acrobats and around a hundred elephants decorated in colourful lights. The journey would take us through the capital, Colombo, and would take around six hours.

Sitting on the steps was exhilarating, and an amazing way to see the stunning west coast scenery, towns and villages.

About half an hour from Colombo a man came and tapped me on the shoulder indicating that he was getting off in Colombo and one of us could have his seat. My girlfriend wanted to keep sitting on the stairs, but my bony bum was somewhat numb, so I took the opportunity.

A short while after leaving Colombo a woman sitting nearby indicated that her seat would be vacant at the next stop. There was then an amazing shuffling of seats by the passengers to ensure that my girlfriend and I could sit together.

We ended up in a section with a young boy and girl and their parents. The little girl, who was about eight or nine, had one of the prettiest faces I have ever seen, with gorgeous big brown eyes. She was absolutely mesmerised by my blonde, tanned Aussie girlfriend and could not take her eyes off her. You see, in those days during the war, there were not many blonde people in Sri Lanka.

A short while after we sat down the family opened the food they had brought along for the journey and insisted that we share it with them. We had a wonderful few hours chatting, laughing and learning a little about them and their beautiful country.

As we approached Kandy they asked us to take a photo of the group. They could not afford a camera and gave us their email address so that we could send them the photo. It was one of the most satisfying emails I have ever sent.

Travelling in Kuala Lumpur

'Start the race now' the police commander ordered in a rather agitated tone as the first light of dawn touched the Kuala Lumpur skyline and nearly 4,000 expectant cyclists stood on the start line.

As Race Director I had delayed the start by about 15minutes because my team on the road had radioed me to indicate that the course was not completely traffic free. It was our practice in Singapore, where my business was based, and also other cities that I had worked in, not to start an event until the route was completely 'locked down'.

The traffic police in Malaysia are vastly experienced in professional cycling events, having successfully delivered the le Tour de Langkawi, a race similar to the world famous Tour de France, for many years. And their success, as is common in professional events, was based on closing roads on a rolling basis a short while before the peloton of riders arrived.

I was concerned that, for the safety of the thousands of recreational cyclists, the road should be completely traffic free before we even started. But the traffic police were confident that they would clear the roads using their tried and tested method. Clearly a stand-off with the traffic commander in my first ever event in Malaysia was not going to get me far. So I took a deep, very nervous breath and the ride was flagged off.

Whilst there were a few nerve-wracking moments, the inaugural event was a success and the cyclists loved the opportunity to ride on closed roads through the heart of the stunning city.

Both parties learned some valuable lessons, and the partnership flourished in subsequent years as we worked together to help achieve each other's objectives.

And the morals are...

Some of the key things all of this has taught me, that I want to pass on as advice to you my grandchildren are:

- It is not all about money
- The most comfortable seat doesn't always offer the best view

- Where there is bad there is also usually good – just look for it
- Respect local knowledge and culture
- There may well be another way to do it that will achieve the same outcome
- Offer up your seat
- Share your meals
- Follow up when you say you will
- Walk or ride whenever you can
- Enjoy the experience with your naked eye – not always through the camera lens
- Step out of the fast lane and take the slow train from time to time
- See the world through the eyes of children
- Watch the sun rise and savour the morning light
- If you just walk on by you may be missing the opportunity to make a difference – even if there is some risk involved
- Partnership is key
- Know when to let go
- Give simple gifts
- Enjoy the view
- It is not all about money (and yes, I have deliberately repeated this lesson)

Wishing you safe and happy travels.

Give to yourself, give to others, give globally

Based in Australia, Chris is:

- A business owner, teacher and 'student' who loves to have good quality conversations, gaining new perspectives and helping to bring about a greater conscious awareness for everyone
- Founder of Balance Central – she has worked in the Wellness Industry for over 17 years, and is one of the highest qualified practitioners in her field
- Through Balance Central and her workshops and presentations she loves to work with people who are ready to recognize the recurring patterns that are holding them back in their life and business – and she helps them to achieve greater success through increasing their awareness and creating more balance in their life
- Author of the book 'Balance Central'
- Nominated for the B1G1 Overall Impact Award 2016 and a B1G1 Business for Good Champion

Here is the advice she would give to her grandchildren...

Better business

Business, for me, has been a journey of personal development. Investing in my business is a way of investing in myself. Every day my business highlights my strengths and weaknesses, which by default pushes me through and beyond my comfort zones and helps me harness my own natural abilities. As a result, I am always creating more, designing more and looking for new ways to respond to what my audience and clients are looking for.

Starting a business is such a buzz, the passion and excitement of sharing our offering carries us easily through any challenges. It is a fantastic time as we tune into our personal strengths and do the things that are fun and easy. This buzz is the thing that gets us out of bed and the thing that keeps us going when we feel we are under achieving.

Soon though, this buzz can dwindle - the love and passion is still there – but something disengages, we seem to lose some of our natural motivation. This moment is crucial in any business as it is a turning point and often we need to find a fresh way of igniting our passion, finding a new motivation. Like all things new we need to learn and engage in different ways of thinking, new approaches and new ways of expressing ourselves.

In my own journey I discovered a unique way of finding new motivation, this ignited my original passion with more depth and more motivation than ever before. What I did was looked beyond what I was good at and started to pay attention to what I needed to learn. The most surprising thing for me was how revealing the experience was and how difficult it was to take a look at myself.

I started by recognising my natural strength of organisation, planning and self-discipline. Then I began identifying the areas I was not strong in – new ideas, starting something I hadn't done or seen before and communicating my real value. This was a tough process because it made me face up to the things I still needed to learn.

As much as we find it difficult to admit what we are not good at, identifying so called 'weaknesses' can be a turning point in reigniting the passion and finding new motivation. By focusing on the things we are not as good at, we find a new level of self-acceptance and then a desire to attract that skill towards us. It is at this time we begin attracting people, organisations and opportunities who help and provide a counter weight to our perceived weaknesses.

When we take ownership of the idea that 'we are not good at EVERYTHING' we let others in. We let in ideas and opportunities that build more strength into our business than we had in the beginning. When we fully accept that we need help we can embrace these new opportunities and take our business to a whole new level. Our original passion is boosted as it is being driven by our own strengths and the strengths of others.

Ultimately a business is a vehicle which allows you to express and share your uniqueness - that something that only you can offer. When you engage with yourself – both in strength and weakness - you can complete any hurdle placed in front of you. By acknowledging that you are not good at everything you can identify where you need support to make your business grow. As you continue to identify where growth is needed and open yourself to new ideas your business will keep growing and expanding.

Being open to identifying our 'weaknesses' and accepting help is the formula that keeps a business achieving all that is possible.

> 'Our greatest legacy is created from identifying and
> utilising the strengths that surround us.'

Better life

Uniqueness is a word I use to identify what makes us who we are. It is a combination of that special thing we are born and with, and also the experiences we collect throughout our life.

Standing in my uniqueness is one of the things I strive for in my life. Life has thrown me many curveballs and I have had to find very different ways of coping, it is through all of my experiences that I have become the unique being that I am.

I grew up in a dysfunctional family environment and was forced to find ways to cope with the stress I faced. The primary coping strategy was to conform, to fade a little into the background and to do only what was necessary to survive. In some ways this was a blessing as it taught me to get on with things without being distracted with what was around me – which is a great strength for me even today. However, once I entered adulthood I found that, while these strategies were valuable, they did create some limitations. My learned behaviour was restricting me in what I could achieve. I started to attend many workshops, learnt many new tools and discovered new skills. But found I would take in only some of the information, and then attempt to bring it into my default learned behaviour.

As my self-awareness grew I was able to combine some of my copying strategies with new ideas and my true strengths shone through. My ability to do only what was necessary allowed me to be focused and deliberate in my actions. When I combined this learnt behaviour with my new found information, tools and skills I was able to use only the information that I truly resonated with. I found this combination has helped me to live a life that is perfectly designed for me. My dysfunctional childhood gave me life skills to choose what I need - and then to do things in my own way, regardless of how different that may be to how anyone else appears to achieve things in their life.

We all learn ways of coping in childhood, regardless of our family circumstances. A large part of early childhood is about conforming. We are asked to dress suitably, speak properly and behave appropriately. Conforming to what is expected satisfies our need to be accepted. But, at the same time, it can take away our ability to feel like an individual.

Then we move into our teenage years and we begin discovering emotions, attraction and who we want to be. We want things that our friends have, we want to dress like them and behave like the people who we think are important. The teenage years are vital in our development because we begin discovering what we love and what we don't love. These are the years we are getting to know our self, our emotions and what we really want in life. We simply want to be accepted by our peers as one of the crowd, we want to fit in.

When we reach adulthood we are told to find our own dream and to design our own life.

But this can be difficult because we are used to conforming, fitting in and being accepted as part of the crowd. And now we are being asked to stand out and make our own way in the world. Sometimes we have an added element that the life we are choosing only exists to satisfy others – it's not really our dream – but we choose it because of obligation.

As we come to acknowledge what we want for our life, and accept that we are one of a kind, we begin the discovery of our own dreams and begin to forge our own life. When we finally find a sense of our unique dream we discover the road is much easier, opportunities appear out of nowhere and we can more easily find our way. We have re-gained our uniqueness, that combination of the special thing we are born with and the experiences we have collected along the way. And with this we can create our own reality.

As I continue on this journey that is MY life I rely more and more on my own unique way of seeing the world. As I discover what brings me joy I continue the transformation back to myself. I have learnt to trust and believe in myself. I proudly stand as the unique individual that I am.

> 'We distract ourselves by comparing ourselves to others. Instead look for your uniqueness. Magic always comes from uniqueness.'

Better world

To make the world a better place we need to embrace the concept of giving. To achieve this, we first need to give to ourselves. Then give to those directly around us. And finally, give on a global scale.

For me the idea of giving to myself used to feel selfish, I never felt I deserved it and would often feel guilty if I took time out just for me. When I finally gave myself permission to give to myself I started with something a little unusual. I started by accepting a compliment someone gave me. For years I would brush compliments aside, shake my head and think that the person didn't really mean what they said. When I made a conscious decision to really hear the compliment my thinking started to change and I could finally let go of the guilt of choosing something just for me.

Receiving and giving are very closely associated, so for me being able to receive was my starting point. I then moved to giving to myself in small ways and then naturally I started to value myself. I now give to myself every day and embrace the moments and joy that giving brings.

By giving to myself I naturally give to others, it's no longer a choice, it's something I do and it brings me a great sense of satisfaction to know I have given without conditions. I continue this theme on a global scale and this brings to me the knowledge that somewhere, someone has been positively impacted by my giving and I know that I have made a difference.

You may find that, like me, giving to yourself feels uncomfortable, something negative, something that you don't deserve. The key is to first realise that you are valuable, remember you are the sum of all of your experiences, all of your perspectives and all of your self-learnings, and that is what makes you valuable. Your learnings and your wisdom are vital for the people around you - they really do need the best version of you.

When you value yourself you give space to make self-improvements. As you learn more about yourself you begin to more easily see the value you bring to others, which also builds on the value you hold within yourself. The cycle continues and you have more and more to give.

When you become practiced in valuing and giving to yourself you naturally gain a capacity to give to others. And then, when you consciously decide to give to someone else, you will often find that you are rewarded in exchange. Sometimes it will be by a direct 'Thank You' and sometimes it will come in the form of someone else offering to give something to you.

It can be difficult to work out what others might need, we don't want to give for the sake of giving, we want it to be meaningful. Sometimes we feel that what others want most is material things or money, and we are not always in a position to give in that way. In fact, giving to others can be as simple as listening, asking how someone is feeling, making a phone call, dropping in on a neighbour. And, when you give of yourself, the value you give to that person is priceless. Just the simple act of listening and showing up creates a ripple effect of giving and receiving value.

Expanding the process of giving to the global arena can feel overwhelming because there is so much needed and we are just one person. How can we really be making a difference? We can feel like we don't have enough to give to make a substantial difference. The truth is that each small gift of giving makes a difference.

These gifts may be financial, or they may be something much greater than money or possessions - we can give a little of our self through volunteering or giving to a charity. Giving globally is about giving with no expectation of receiving in return except for knowing that we have created a change in the world.

Giving is the greatest thing we can do for ourselves, others and the world at large.

When we give to ourselves we create an opening to give to others. When we give to others we feel that we have made a difference in someone else's life. When we give globally we realise we have created real change in the world.

Achieving a sense of giving starts with giving just one tiny thing every day – start with yourself and the rest will come naturally.

'Give of yourself without expectation and you will receive riches you cannot even imagine.'

Face and move past your fears

Based in Australia, Craigh:

- Is a medical and business intuitive, healer, author, thought leader and keynote speaker
- Teaches people to heal their personal and business blocks and create heart based abundance
- Is the author of the 2017 book 'Intuitive', which has received excellent pre-release reviews
- Serves a client base that includes international entrepreneurs and global Fortune 2000 executives and companies
- Craigh and his clients have been featured by Forbes, Inc, The New York Times, The Huffington Post, CNN, BBC World News and on stage at TEDx

Here is the advice he would give to his grandchildren...

Better business

Do what you love. Happiness, money and success will then follow you. The more you love what you do, and the more people it helps, the more successful you will be. The world will truly be a better place by you loving what you do.

Sounds so simple, doesn't it?

But it takes courage to do what you love. Character and true grit, to find out who you truly are and to live it. Nobody else on the planet, not even your partner, parents, siblings or best friends can tell you how you truly feel inside. What your unique passions, skills and talents are.

Honour your truth. Honour how you truly feel. Be an example to others by doing what you love. Inspire the world by your actions and the true joy of totally loving what you do. Loving what you do is the most unselfish thing you can do. It provides freedom for you and all those around you to truly be themselves. To be fully expressed in your chosen career and or business.

I promise you this: if you follow the journey of doing what you love, you will never regret it and you will never work another day for the rest of your life.

If you don't know what you love, that's OK. Don't be too hard on yourself. The hardest thing for most people is finding what they truly love to do. Be patient, give yourself time. It took me until my early thirties to start really moving towards what I love to do. Keep trying and tweaking things you like doing and are passionate about, until you really know.

It's not a race.

If you are honest with yourself, you will eventually be able to condense it down to three to five things. Try one out and see how it goes. Give it your best. And if it is not as much fun doing it as you thought... move on to the next.

This is what worked for me. I have been doing what I really love for nearly ten years now and have never looked back. I will keep doing what I love, health and body willing, well into my seventies and beyond. I am not interested in retiring, I am interested in doing as much as I can for other people. Leaving a legacy for others to follow to help the health and well-being of people and heart-based businesses on our planet.

Today, more than ever before, young people are looking to work for themselves or in a business that they are truly passionate about. Doing what you love is not only a good idea for you - it is also a great idea for your customers. And it is excellent for your health and your overall well-being.

When you are passionate about what you do, it feels much less like work. When facing difficult challenges in the business - which will come - you will be more determined to face and overcome those challenges head on. If it is just a job to pay the bills and get by, you will only try so hard. If you are only doing it for the money, the happiness will only be there when the money is there.

This is one of the biggest lessons I learned.

In my earlier career I told myself, I will make a bunch of money by the time I am twenty-five and then I will do what I truly love. I did make a bunch of money, had some incredible experiences and spent a bunch of money too.

Then when I was twenty-five I said when I am thirty and make a huge amount of money then I will do what I really want to do.

The pattern repeated.

I did make a huge amount of money and spent a huge amount of money to get the business to a certain stage turning over multi millions of dollars. By the time I was heading towards my early thirties, my health, stress levels, happiness and personal life were really suffering.

I knew it was now or never. So I made a big decision. I bit the bullet, took action and never looked back.

It was not easy. It was the hardest and most rewarding decision of my life. I did not want to be thirty-five having the same conversation with myself.

When you love what you do and are truly living your dream you are more likely to do whatever it takes to succeed. To not only be a better company, but be the best person you can be.

If you compare your life and your success to others, you are doing a great disservice to yourself and to them. Most people not only don't like what they do, they actually secretly hate it. Deep inside their life force is dimming, working longer and longer hours with less job security than ever before, doing something they don't want to do. Life is too short and goes way too fast. Don't do it. Go on the adventurous journey of finding and doing business based around what you really love.

When you love what you do, you begin to beam with happiness. You glow with enthusiasm about what you do and how it helps and improves the lives of others.

Having tried several careers in my life over many years, when I finally decided what I truly wanted to do in my mid-thirties my life changed for ever. When I stopped working for money, when I stopped working for other people out of fear, and when I stopped worrying about what other people thought... I was the happiest I had ever been.

Don't look back on your life in old age and say 'I should have done something else'.

Don't look back on your life with regret.

Start being grateful for where you are at right now. Be excited that you are at the beginning of an amazing journey. That you know you are moving towards having the ultimate business.

You don't have to change overnight. If you are willing to, then fantastic, congratulations. If not, like most of us, you can make your passion a hobby or a part time job as I did. Over many years I did more and more of what I wanted to do. Starting on the weekends then three days a week, then four then five. You get the idea. When you can replace your income with what you really love to do, I believe you have truly made it.

The best thing you can do right now is make a commitment to yourself that you are going to do what you love.

Take some action towards it. No matter how small or large. Your life will change dramatically for the better.

If you are doing what you love, then my advice to you (and to myself) is to do more of it. Make it better for your customers and you will experience a true ten-fold return. Seeing the loving smiles on their faces because of the joy you bring to their lives through your business. Why? Because you truly love what you do and they can feel it and will want to keep buying from you because of it.

Better life

Always come from your heart. Our own heart is where life is truly at.

Now, come on a wonderful journey with me... Remember a time, right now, when you were truly free and happy. Remember where you were, your age, the weather that day and who were you with. How it felt, to be free and feel truly safe. You are now in a very loving place, you are smiling and you truly know, in your heart, that anything is possible. Come now from your heart, with love for your family, friends and for yourself.

When we live a heart-based life, we glow from the inside out. We are aligned with our values; we are aligned with our truth. We are not trying to be anything we are not. We are being as honest as we can be with ourselves and our interactions with others. We are coming from a place of love first. A place that is unconditional. Not conditional.

When you live life from a place of 'I will do this for you if you do this for me', you are not being heart-based. You are being conditional. Most societies in our world are sadly structured this way. Modern society has been about the rise of the individual. About competition. It is coming from a place of lacking where there can only be one winner.

Coming from the heart is an abundant place. There is a place and a space for you and others to be truly heard. Room for a society to connect at the deepest levels of love through our hearts.

When we are unconditional, when we give what we can - not giving too much, not giving too little - we are now coming from a fair place of exchange. We are loving others and ourselves equally.

I teach people, executives, CEOs and world leaders this very transformational way of being. When I mention the word 'love' I do not mean the romantic notion of love. The love I am talking about is universal. The love from a parent to a child. The love of doing something for a stranger without the need for recognition. The joy knowing that in some small or large way you have truly impacted the lives of another person or community.

When we come from our heart, it removes the need to come from fear. Fear is a natural part of the human condition. It has its uses. For example, it is very easy to over think situations, I know when I am in fear I over think. Being too much in our heads takes us out of heart and the power of our positive feelings of trust, intuition and knowing that everything will be OK. Of course, we still need to be responsible for living from a place of an open heart. Boundaries are important and can be learned over time.

If we are constantly living life from a place of logic and cognitive processing, we are missing out on the opportunity of an emotionally rich life. Missing the opportunity not only to connect deeply with life and with others. Most importantly missing the opportunity to connect deeply with ourselves.

When we live by our truth aligned with our values, we can more easily take stock of ourselves. Being heart-based will certainly not make you perfect. It is a lifestyle that develops over time. As we learn more about life and ourselves we have the opportunity to see if we are truly growing as a person. Adjusting our values and feelings to a higher standard. Potentially living with more understanding and compassion for others and, over time, for ourselves.

Living a heart-based life provides you with the real opportunity to connect on a deeper level to others and society at large. It allows you use more of your senses to feel life more and more. When we are on holidays we are generally happier and slower to pass judgement on others and on ourselves. This is the opportunity of living life from your heart. It is a loving place of giving, of allowing, of understanding and of forgiving. It allows the opportunity for you to show the best version of yourself to others and for others in return to show the best version of themselves back to you. The Universe becomes a mirror, reflecting back to you who you are being and how you are feeling,

The most important thing about living your life from your heart is that you are doing your best every day. That way, in the end, everything will be OK because most of the things we worry about in life never happen. Life is to be lived and to be enjoyed.

When you live a heart-based life you give permission for others to live this way too.

Having travelled all over the world in nearly 100 cities, I can tell you that we are mostly all the same. People are more alike than not alike. We want what is best for our families, friends and society at large. It is only when we are in a fearful or unhappy place that we don't want what is best for others.

Being heart-based you will create heart-based relationships, personally, with the general public and in business. You will never fully know the difference it makes to others. The smile that you gave to homeless person in the street, the single mother struggling to make ends meet and just get by. You may have been the only genuine person who smiled at them or said hello to them in a week, a month or even longer.

Live a heart-based life for the difference it will make - not only to you, to your family and friends, but also to the world around you.

Better world

Give. There it is.

One simple word, and perhaps the most powerful the planet. The answer to the question, and the solution to the problem, in just four letters.

The best way to make the world a better place is to give. To give first. To give period. For you, me and all of us on the planet to give to others. No matter how small or how big.

For me, the game of humanity is giving.

Now I would like to share something with you about my journey of giving. Thinking back and remembering growing up as a child, what would you hear, what would I hear?

We heard wise sages saying it is 'better to give than to receive', didn't we?

In many western societies giving first can be a very hard concept to fathom. Honestly, most of us in the developed world, take our quality of life very much for granted. Living in a peaceful country, having relative economic security, the warmth of personal relationships. And owning many unnecessary possessions.

Of course, there is nothing wrong with having nice things. The point is that we receive, but we are not grateful for what we are receiving. Nor are we grateful for what we already have.

There is a hunger for something more, whatever it is. Not having enough. That more is somehow better.

However, sometimes having more for yourself means less for another.

If we are all connected, all humans, now proven scientifically as well as spiritually, by giving less to others who is the one truly worst off? Not that people are inherently greedy or mean-spirited. More likely that we are not conscious of the abundance that we already have. Not only to enjoy for ourselves but to share generously with others.

When you give, and you give whole heartedly without *any* expectation of receiving, just for the pure joy of giving... that is when it is truly better to give than to receive.

There are so many ways to give.

To give a smile, a warm hand shake, hugs, a compliment. One of the most powerful gifts you can give, much more than money, is time. To be present with someone. In the moment. To listen and allow them to share with you a problem, a concern or an achievement. Even more importantly, they share their hopes and dreams with you.

I have learned over the years that, apart from the necessities of food and shelter, most human beings crave two things: to be heard and to be understood.

'I hear what you are saying, I see what you mean, thank you for sharing with me.' We don't necessarily have to agree with the person we are listening too. We don't necessary even need to like them or have them like you. If we can be generous enough to *truly* listen to a person, to provide them a space, have them heard, miracles can and do happen.

Most people don't want handouts - or even ask for them.

Most people want to be loved and have some love for themselves. This comes through achievement. Of small and large goals. Through empowerment. The old saying 'teach a child how to fish and they will be able to fish forever' comes to mind. Human beings have unlimited potential. Don't steal their potential by just doing it for them. Believe in them. See them bigger than they see themselves. More importantly, listen to them. Really listen.

You cannot help everyone. But help who you can. You can be there when they are ready and willing to receive and to succeed.

When we give, and give with the joy of truly helping another, it is the greatest gift in the world. It gives you a warm tingling feeling you cannot explain. It makes you feel whole, complete. That there is nothing to do or be, except to enjoy the act of giving to another. To connect with their spirit and to know that you have made their life and the world a little (or perhaps even a lot) better today.

For me, giving is becoming a way of living.

Not because I seek acknowledgement for it. To be honest, for me the best form of giving is to give without anyone knowing about it. To give so frequently and often that you forget your acts of giving and that those acts of giving change a person's life for ever without you knowing.

As my personal life and business evolves I feel more comfortable with my own success, knowing that every action in my business results in a giving – via the B1G1 Business for Good giving platform - that makes a real difference to people's lives.

And as I become happier with my life, and more prosperous in so many ways, I am able to help others more. More frequently, consistently and deeply.

So my advice to you is to give.

It makes my heart truly sing and shine brightly. And I know it will do the same for you.

The answer is to become a social entrepreneur

Originally from Australia, and now based in the UK, Daniel is:

- Co-founder of Dent Global, which has offices in the UK, US, Singapore, and Australia serving over 2000 business leader clients
- Creator of the Key Person of Influence programme
- Author of the best-selling business books 'Oversubscribed', 'Entrepreneur revolution' and 'Key person of influence'
- And was named as one of the most influential entrepreneurs in the UK on the Power List 100

Here is the advice he would give to his grandchildren...

Three core problems

The world is transforming rapidly and many people feel a sense of anxiety about the future. They worry about their own lives and being able to achieve and experience all the fruits of life. They worry about their countries and the vast economic challenges that are emerging. Naturally, most people also worry about the planet and our ability to sustain the lives of over 7.5 billion people.

And those worries are well founded, because the future will be defined by three core problems:

1 - The existential crisis - Every human being has a deep yearning for meaning and impact to prove their life is worth something. Never before in history have we had to worry about our personal impact potential. For tens of thousands of years most humans (with a few Royal exceptions) had no ability to impact the world. They couldn't travel very far, they couldn't communicate with many others and they had virtually no strategies to improve life. Most humans never consumed anything that could harm the environment, and simply weren't aware of what other humans were collectively doing beyond their own village.

But now that we can travel, we can start successful ventures, we can communicate with millions of people and we are aware of our impact on the planet, we each feel a deep sense of personal responsibility to make the most of this potential and to improve the world we live in.

2 - The economic crisis - The economy is based upon traditions and insights from the past that are no longer relevant. The notion of 'countries' is outdated, the idea that people need to work to keep society running is coming to its end, and the idea that money is issued as a never-ending cycle of debt is being questioned.

All of this is tearing at the fabric of our economy; neither governments nor bankers have a clue on how to transform things. We have the technology to feed and clothe every person on earth - and yet the current economic paradigm creates a bottleneck that prevents it happening. Clearly there are big issues around inequality, happiness and harming the planet that can only be solved by improving our economic model.

3 - The ecological crisis - The world is dangerously close to a systemic collapse that could cause a mass extinction for humanity. It's linked to the way we produce energy, the way we dispose of waste, the way we treat nature and the way we divide up land. If we continue to run things the way we currently do, the extinction of some species is almost inevitable before this century is over. For example, if a significant number of people want shark-fin soup we will wipe out the apex predator of the ocean. And the consequences of that are unthinkable.

But small changes can have huge effects – as we saw in the UK when the government introduced a small tax on plastic bags and dramatically reduced their consumption (and waste) in a matter of months. As a species we have to be smart about protecting our own habitat. We have the technology and the resources to fix the issues - but we need the political willpower to match it.

A single solution for better businesses, better lives and a better world

The wonderful news is that all three of these problems are linked and can be solved in unison. There's a way for people to simultaneously derive a personal sense of meaning, improve the global economy and repair our habitat in time for us to survive.

Every individual must become a social entrepreneur.

They must link their enterprise to acts of good that improve the planet and society. Through social entrepreneurship individuals create the businesses of the future, fund important projects and become an engine for improving the planet.

This answers the existential crisis too – the sense of purpose derived from social entrepreneurship silences the inner voice that nags for important work to do.

Humans are built to make the most of their surroundings in a way that benefits our tribe and ourselves. We derive the most meaning from a blend of personal success and doing the right thing by others. A person who has a successful business and is also improving an aspect of the environment or society, is someone who has a deep sense of purpose and meaning in their life.

The mission of my organisation, Dent Global, is to help create 'a world full of entrepreneurial people solving meaningful problems'. In the early stages of business that often means generating leads, funding for growth and improving the product or service. Once these challenges are solved, the meaningful problems revolve around linking the business to the right charitable projects.

Many entrepreneurs have discovered that a business doing good grows faster than a business run purely for profit. When a business has a social cause it attracts dynamic people to its team - and customers feel better about buying from a company that's doing great things in the world. Even if you don't have an altruistic bone in your body, there are plenty of reasons to solve more meaningful problems.

Of course there are very few entrepreneurs who don't have a social conscience.

Entrepreneurship requires a deep sense of empathy to put yourself in the shoes of a customer and to effectively lead a team. This empathy eventually creeps up on you and causes you to search for bigger problems to solve.

Over the past five years we've built a global business. We've attracted investment at a high valuation, hired world-class professionals below their competitive rate and we've become a preferred supplier with big companies who normally don't use smaller providers. A key ingredient for these achievements is the strong sense of purpose that's embedded into our culture.

From day one we found ways to give and to raise money for charity. We found charities that support entrepreneurs in developing countries and that help the environment. We also encouraged our 2000+ clients to do the same - and many of them have joined us as supporters of the B1G1 Business For Good movement (www.b1g1.com).

Giving to charity and raising money sharpens your entrepreneurial skills and strengthens your sense of purpose. It's never been easier to get the benefits of giving thanks to B1G1; they select powerful projects, they track and measure the impact and they help companies demonstrate their commitment to customers and team members.

Giving is an awesome strategy - and if we all do it we will achieve success individually and collectively.

Continuously learn about the world and yourself

Based in Malaysian Borneo, David:

- Is a creative teambuilding expert who leads a dynamic multinational learning organisation
- Designs and delivers highly impactful team alignment activities across the Asia Pacific region
- Is originally from Wales in the UK, but has lived and worked in South East Asia for 25 years

Here is the advice he would give to his grandchildren...

Better business

Far too often our main focus of training and development, in ourselves and others, is to mitigate a lack of understanding or capability in areas of weakness. While of course we are all required to perform at least at a base level of competence, there is an opportunity for superior performance and a huge injection of positive energy that usually does not cost anything!

In 25 years of facilitating team development at organisations around the world, I have found a key and often untapped common denominator. This is the opportunity to make massive improvements in both individual and team performance through a focus on supporting everyone to identify, be proud of, develop and utilise their unique talents.

Recognise, value, develop and use your own talents, and the talents of others. Closely examine yourself - using self-reflection, feedback and even diagnostic tests - in order to name, describe and own your talents. Once you have recognised these talents, consider carefully how these talents already add value. It is a very interesting, and often rather mind blowing, exercise to put a monetary value on this talent and therefore the potential return if this specific talent is developed and used more. Given what is often a huge potential return, the next steps - i.e. further developing your talents and creating clear and executable action plans to use them more - are very exciting.

Liberate your own talents and experience the powerful impact. Very quickly I am sure you will also become an advocate of talent liberation and help others also liberate their own talents. The opportunity is immense!

Better life

Where and how the incredible journey that is life takes us, is determined by many things. While it may often feel you are not in total control, or at times are barely in control at all, there is one single person that is setting and steering the direction of your life... and that is you, yourself. The multitude of choices that you face every hour, day, month, year and decade - some barely noticeable, some instantly life changing - each combine to set your life's direction.

My advice is very simple to say and rather more difficult to implement - which is whenever possible TAKE THE TOUGHER CHOICE.

At any moment there will often be a tempting, and often totally acceptable, option that is drawing you towards it. At least it is totally acceptable to almost everyone (your family, colleagues, community, society etc.), except the most important person - the only person taking that specific expedition that is your life - you!

To you it will often indeed be acceptable but quite possibly not *totally* acceptable - there will be a little question of doubt in your head about what is down that other path.

Growing your awareness around what you are deciding, how you are choosing and just stepping out and taking that slightly less easy option will have a huge impact. Many years ago I was travelling through Borneo and happened to hear about the only Outdoor Education centre in the country. I was already interested in experiential education and loved the outdoors, so I thought I would drop by and visit for a couple of hours to see how it was carried out in such a different environment and climate than I was used to (hill walking and camping in the freezing rain of the Welsh mountains springs to mind).

This was before the internet and Google map. All I had was the name of the village the centre was named after. So I hopped on a little local minibus to that village. All was good until we arrived there and I discovered (with a little pointing and waving and my, at that stage, very basic Malay language) that the outdoor centre was actually another 6km further down the road. The bus driver turned around and offered me a free ride back into town and the comfort of where I was staying.

However at that moment I took the tougher choice, and hopped out of the bus onto the side of the road. I was in the middle of nowhere, not really having any idea of where I was heading for - but decided to hitchhike in what normally would be thought of as the 'wrong' direction (i.e. away from all that I knew about). Someone quickly stopped - somewhat surprising, as I found out later that no one hitchhiked in Borneo - and took me the extra distance.

The rest is a very long story - as it really was a life-determining destination - and in the 25 years since I have built a business, family and life all directly related to taking that tough choice.

To this day I can still recollect exactly how close I was to taking the easy option of staying on the comfortable bus back to the place I knew, when my life would have been so totally different in almost every way.

The next tougher choice might be a conversation it would be much easier not to have, giving someone some feedback that they may not like, asking for advice from someone, buying or indeed not buying something, reacting in a collaborative way, trying a different behaviour, saying no to something you do not feel is right, or pushing yourself a little harder than previously... whatever it is... make that tough choice!

Better world

SEE IT and truly LIVE IN IT - preferably in as many different parts of the world as possible.

SEEK to UNDERSTAND the multitude of diverse behaviours, habits, preferences, beliefs and attitudes that you will meet. Be surprised or shocked by, marvel at and sometimes just shake your head in disbelief at them.

There are so many stunningly beautiful places to visit in the world, and do take every chance to experience as many amazing environments as you can. But I urge you to in addition to enjoying the physical locations, focus on getting to know, and understanding, your fellow members of this global society.

I had a wonderful childhood growing up in a beautiful part of West Wales and still love to go back and visit. However that very phrase - going back - truly describes the reality after more than 25 years of being fortunate enough to live and work in a culture and society so different and yet also equally wonderful. In fact, I am certain that the exposure and immersion in different cultures, a different religion, different climate and even the wonders of totally different favourite foods all add to a deeper understanding and appreciation of my 'original' culture. I hugely enjoy the powerful opportunity to blend these differences together into what could be called my personal culture.

Open your mind, seize opportunities to work, live, play, converse and share with as many different characters and cultures as you can – the benefit to you, and to each of them, is immense. In addition such understanding and awareness is no doubt making the world a better place.

The other vital part of the equation is to SEEK to be UNDERSTOOD, by proactively sharing with others what makes you so wonderfully, uniquely you.

Think deeply about what makes you the unique citizen of our world - your roots, happenings in your life, the society and culture (or hopefully the numerous societies and cultures) you have been immersed in, and take every opportunity you can to openly share and teach others about all of these.

I live in Malaysia where everyone takes their shoes off before going into their own or anyone else's house. This is such a norm that it is automatic, almost unconscious behaviour. However in many other parts of the world it would be very unusual for someone to take their shoes off before entering the house. In fact when I visit some other countries and still automatically slip off my shoes at the front door - my host often looks surprised. On one occasion a relative even went off on a tirade against dog owners who walk their pets and do not clean up after them - putting my shoe removal action together with a thought of why they might take this action themselves, and coming up with a potentially smelly conclusion!

The reverse is true when people from different - lets call them 'non shoe slipping' cultures - come to visit Asia. I learnt the wonderful benefit of proactive sharing of cultural norms though the situation of a visitor arriving at our home and happily walking into the house with their shoes on, as is their normal behaviour. A look of disbelief flashes across the faces of those in the house and then there is an instant of uncomfortable indecision. Do I keep quiet so as not to risk making the visitor feel uncomfortable, but then they still have their shoes on for the rest of their stay and we feel uncomfortable? Or do I ask them to go back to the front door and remove their shoes, trying very hard not to make it sound as though they have done something wrong?

The best solution for everyone in this simple situation, but also in a multitude of others, is being consciously proactive in gently teaching the other party something they almost certainly do not know. In my case, as we walk from the car towards the front door, I say clearly 'in Asia we always take our shoes off before entering the house and you can place your shoes just over there'

So my simple advice is... don't wait to be asked... instead GIVE by teaching and sharing as much as possible about yourself, your culture, your habits and preferences. Painless and yet powerful sharing.

The whole is greater than the sum of the parts (...but only if you share)

Based in Australia, Deborah:

- Sees her primary role as family – and her husband and five young adults are at the core of her 'why'
- In business she seeks to enhance the lives of other families
- Her brand, Decisions Plus, is all about collaborating with business owners who, at their core, share her vision that ours is a world of abundance if we only share
- She is a passionate supporter of the UN Sustainable Development Goal 17 – Revitalize the global partnership for sustainable development

Here is the advice she would give to her grandchildren...

Better business

Collaboration produces an effect where the combined impact is greater than the sum of the parts – it's called synergy.

Traditional business models would have us believe that we should cling to every competitive advantage, putting our own business first and revelling in the belief that we could attain 100% market share. Then newer models were created that suggested we could collaborate in partnerships of mutual gain – once again to truly secure 100% market share.

But why do we want 100% market share? Surely there is such an eclectic group of customers that we couldn't possibly serve their needs...

...and of course that is what happens. Service loses out, a competitor steps in and no-one ever gains 100% of the market.

The problem is, these models of thought are based around the idea that there is scarcity – that there could never be enough for everyone. But what if that whole premise is wrong... what if we acted from the conviction that there is an abundance of everything and the only ingredient missing is sharing.

This era is seeing the rise of collaboration and the sharing economy - not only with partnerships but with competitors. It will be interesting to look back in 20 years when this current school of thought is 'old-fashioned' and see what new and exciting opportunities have been imagined.

I truly believe, however, that once business owners break the mindset of viewing everything in terms of scarcity and instead focus on how to build abundance we will never go back.

My advice? Every time you find yourself thinking about what you don't have, remind yourself that it is time to share what you do have.

Better life

Dreams are what we do while we are asleep – they are involuntary – they are sensations or ideas or images or ideas that our brain picks up and puts down at random.

A vision, however, is about

- Being able to see
- Being able to plan for the future, and
- Being able to view the future with imagination.

Life goals - our aspirations and hopes and plans - should not then be referred to as dreams but as our vision.

Vision too should come with a sense of purpose - a drive to pursue that vision in the absolute conviction that to do so will bring about a better world.

You have the absolute capability to solve huge problems, but you need to know which one will be your problem... because that will inspire both your vision and your purpose.

Better world

Never say the following sentence 'You know what you should do...'

If it needs doing, you do it.

- Collaborate
- Inspire

- Do good
- Give in abundance
- Receive with heartfelt thanks
- Be trustworthy
- Be of service

...and do it all with humility.

A week and a bit of world, life and business inspiration

Based in Australia, Guy:

- Has been a General Practitioner in Melbourne for 30 years
- Trained at St Bartholomew's Hospital in London
- Has been widely published in leading medical journals
- Won the Prime Minister's award for Diabetes Management in 2007
- Is on the Diabetes Steering Committee
- Is the married father of three children

Here is the advice he would give to his grandchildren...

Better world

So much to say, and only one chapter to do it.

The opportunity to reflect on various areas of life came in an unexpected way when I was called to the UK to spend time with my gravely ill mother. This prompted a whirlwind ten days encompassing the World, Life and Business, so the challenge of capturing it all in a chapter of a book made perfect sense.

To start off, it was almost a privilege to be in the UK during the immediate aftermath of Brexit and to observe it both subjectively and objectively at a pivotal point of history.

My week in the UK was historic, chaotic and shocking.

Extraordinary does not do those seven days justice. Unimaginable probably does. Not even Jeffrey Archer could have produced a script quite like it.

The UK was grievously divided, split by geography, class, age, levels of education and cultural outlook. The Prime Minister, David Cameron, had resigned. Boris Johnson, who had been odds on favourite to replace Mr Cameron until hours before his nomination, was stabbed in the back by his right hand man and main supporter, The Justice Secretary

Michael Gove, who had promised to help him become Prime Minister. In turn, despite charges of treachery, Michael Gove then declared his own surprise candidacy for Prime Minister. Finally Nigel Farage, the other main face of the Leave campaign, also quit as leader of UK Independence Party, claiming death threats as the cause.

Meanwhile Labour went into meltdown with Jeremy Corbyn, their leader, being pilloried for his lack lustre role in The Remain campaign. He lost a vote of no confidence by his party's MPs by 172 to 40. More than 60 shadow front benchers resigned their posts. In fact, so many quit that 81 year-old MP Paul Flynn reappeared on the front bench for the first time in a quarter of a century to take business questions as Corbyn restocked his shadow cabinet.

Michael Heseltine, The Tory Grandee, eloquently eviscerated Boris Johnson during a BBC interview; 'He has ripped the party apart, and created the greatest constitutional crisis in modern times. He's knocked billions off the value of the nation's savings and is like a general that led his army to the sound of guns and at the sight of battle abandoned the field.'

On a personal basis I have never seen such a rift between my siblings living in England, with each of them supported by their partners as they sat on opposing sides of the debate. This rift seemed only minor when compared to the vitriol expressed by nephews and nieces who were extremely hurt by the vote, and deeply concerned as to how the younger generation were going to deal with it and repair the damage caused in their opinion by the 'selfish baby boomers', the 'uninformed' and the like.

I also have great trepidation for my cousin and family living in Gibraltar, who like many living there are concerned that once Article 50 is triggered that Spain will make it very difficult for them. The Brexit result certainly stopped them buying a house there, and being forced to leave in the future is a distinct possibility.

The full repercussions of Brexit undermining a fragile Europe are yet to be seen, but potentially could have huge ramifications, not just in Europe but for the whole world. Some have even argued that the British passport has suddenly become an item of shame and embarrassment. So much so that three of my nieces are even looking at obtaining Irish passports. This anguish is undoubtedly spread up and down and across the UK, which is seriously fractured.

The general consensus is that Remain would now win a second referendum with estimates that two-thirds of leave voters now believe they were misled by the Leave campaign.

It has become clear that Boris Johnson, Michael Gove and Nigel Farage only supported the Leave campaign to further their own careers.

Truth be told there is a lot of evidence that Boris Johnson's conversion to the Leave campaign was a manipulative ploy, with many speculating that a narrow Remain vote would have actually been his preferable outcome. Then Johnson would have been able to ride the wave of bitter disappointment on the Tory backbenches and taken the leadership from David Cameron without inheriting the mess the country is now in. Criticism is coming in from every direction that Boris Johnson has 'smashed up the place for nothing'.

However, even Boris Johnson and Michael Gove were pawns in a political grand game. In reality it was Rupert Murdoch pulling the strings with his newspaper *The Times* and in cohorts with Paul Dacre at *The Daily Mail*, who employed the journalist wife of Michael Gove, Sarah Vine, to undermine Boris Johnson in an 'Exit Boris' push. Michael Gove was Murdoch's preferred option (puppet) as Prime Minister, but even his tabloids could not turn the tide of anger against Michael Gove by his treachery both to Boris Johnson and David Cameron.

In a disappointing reflection, UK monitors had also recorded an explosion of racial intolerance, stating that the vote has set back multiculturalism 20 years. No wonder Brexit has been welcomed in Europe by European fascist parties, and in the USA by white supremacists and the likes of Donald Trump. It goes to show what happens when the politics of fear are allowed to appeal to parochialism, and it isn't pretty. Well known radio presenters of Asian heritage who have lived in UK all their lives stated that strangers were now coming up to them and telling them to leave. Friends who have relatives living in the UK have also reported similar experiences.

On the Leave front obviously there were false campaigns on the potential benefits of extra National Health Scheme funding & immigration control. There would have been a number of anti-bureaucratic votes due to the sentiment against the belief of the bureaucracy in Brussels living off other people's earnings. Some voted with a degree of unsubstantiated optimism that British trade could 'flourish without the shackles of Brussels', and that the UK could be potentially freed from its EU constraints, and could establish deals with China, India, Japan, South Korea, USA, all the members of the Commonwealth and the rest of the world.

Ironically, even if this did all pan out it may still not be timely enough for many of the older generation who voted for Leave, and it is improbable that it will ever justify the massive political and social havoc it has caused.

Brexit has ripped out the UK's soul. Let's hope that the recovery required occurs as soon and as painlessly as possible, and that those who wanted 'their' country back do not get their wish as it will turn out to be a hostile, inhospitable place for immigrants, ethnic minorities, homosexuals and everyone and anyone who wasn't included when Nigel Farage proclaimed victory for 'ordinary, decent people'. It all sounds ominously similar to the gospel preached amidst the 'Ministry Of Love' in George Orwell's *1984*.

I know these political wounds can one day heal. And I look forward to waking up soon into a good world with a good England. Into a world that advocates solidarity and progression in challenging a climate filled with fear-mongering and scare tactics. On that day, I look forward to proclaiming that I am from the United Kingdom, and that I am proud.

Although recognising the vast differences in circumstances between the issues of immigration into the UK and Australia, hopefully the UK can look at the Australian State of Victoria's model of egalitarianism (as differentiated to other states in Australia) as an example of a way forward.

Essentially the Victorian Multicultural Commission was established in 1983 and the Victorian Government has since passed 'a bill of rights act' for its citizens with a three- pronged approach to immigration. Firstly encouraging and celebrating cultural diversity. Secondly sharing the difference between ethnic groups. And thirdly recognising that we are all Australian citizens.

The Victorian experience has made the change of our society more purposeful. The advantages of a diverse society have been acknowledged and the state's legislation has recognised that. The Victorian Multicultural Commission was established and has the power to encourage the 200 various ethnic groups who make up its society to celebrate their cultures. It regularly makes money available to those groups to allow them to function as social organisations and to publicly celebrate. The money is given with the clear understanding that they will share their celebrations with other people in the society, and as a result Melbourne is a really fun place with its array of multicultural festivals and celebrations.

There is an overarching understanding in all of this that we are all Australian citizens and have a responsibility to maintain Australian laws.

For many years the various Government departments have been required to account for their management in multicultural terms. Annual public meetings are held in which people from the ethnic groups are given the opportunity to comment on how the government has met their needs. Most of those comments have been very positive.

Even in the face of some strenuous anti-Muslim statements in recent times from conservative groups, the well-established acceptance of multiculturalism (not assimilation) is strong in Victoria and I think it works.

My own belief, on both a personal and social scale, is that the idea of being happy with who you are, is essential to being able to accept others and their cultures.

Therefore if I could only pass on one piece of advice to my grandchildren about making the world a better place, it would be:

Be happy with who you are. Eat well, be active, and maintain fruitful relationships with partners, family and friends. Have a belief in something (anything!) Maintain good health and ongoing education. Finally create a career and life with the purpose of good and by being valuable members of your community and the world itself.

Better life

After the week that was Brexit, it was time for reflection at a 'Business for Good' conference in Bali. I would be enjoying great company, energy and purpose and the seeds for this whole book.

I had just arrived at 4am, having come from visiting my poorly mother in Chertsey England. She was in a nursing home, needing a very high level of care after a stroke, which had added to her dementia, failing sight and hearing. To all intents and purposes, at 86 years of age she was dying, living in her worst fears, being completely dependent in a nursing home. A few years earlier, at 79, she had been very social and still swimming, playing tennis and socialising.

During the trip I had managed to thank her and tell her she was appreciated for all the great things she did to help me in my life. She did smile at certain salient points and although limited in expression, it was a surreal and very sad moment when I left her and explained to her that I was returning to Australia at which she shed a tear. The first and the last I will see from her.

Whilst that aspect was difficult, as it always will be, there were positive notes. My youngest son, Matt, came with me and we made it into an awesome week of visiting and reconnecting with family and friends. The goal was to reinforce family bonds, meeting with every one of his cousins. Matt too was making the most of a disappointment having represented Australia at beach handball, both in Columbia 2013 and Brazil 2014, just after the football World Cup. This time he narrowly missed out on selection for the present world championships in Budapest, Hungary. Much like beach volleyball was to volleyball, beach handball is a sport just outside the Olympics. Matt can already claim to having been in Australia's first ever win in a world championship, and was looking forward to playing in an even stronger team who are still improving.

Whilst in Columbia Matt had managed to make it onto the Columbian news in an interview with foreign sport stars at The World Games (for games just outside The Olympics). In great exuberance he proclaimed how he 'loved Columbia', he 'loved the food 'and he 'loved the people' which made him a great hit. What I suspect he didn't say was that he also 'loved his freedom at being away from his parents!'

In Brazil they stayed in the same hotel as the German soccer team, and as the boys explained 'they obviously inspired Germany to thrash the host nation Brazil 7-1' and then to win The World Cup. In the subsequent beach handball, in a televised match against Brazil they were soundly beaten. Brazil eventually became world champions at both beach handball and beach soccer, and apparently as the host nation choose beach soccer over beach handball to be the next new Olympic sport.

So after a week of family gatherings and indeed catching up with all of my nieces and nephews, it was my cousin Nicholas who was the most inspiring. Nicholas is a stuntman appearing in some of the biggest Hollywood blockbusters in recent history, including *Star Wars, Game of Thrones, Harry Potter, Charlie and the Chocolate Factory, Mission Impossible, In The Heart of The Sea and Tarzan* to name just a few. He is now starting life as a young David Attenborough presenting wildlife documentaries from some of the planet's most awesome ecosystems in Borneo and Africa. He is also Ambassador for Orangutan Appeal UK working closely with the Sabah wildlife Department on behalf of the Malaysian government, to raise funds and awareness for both the orangutan now (July 2016) relisted from endangered to critically endangered, and for the Borneo pygmy elephant. He has recently filmed a new awareness campaign to help bring the Borneo pygmy elephant the most endangered elephant in the world, with only 1500 surviving in the wild, back from the brink of extinction.

His excellent and inspirational productions are available to view at www.nicholasdaines.com and are all set to go to educate on some of the world's most endangered species. I also recommend googling 'Nick Daines stuntman' for some amazing stunts too.

Whilst I had been with my mother I also collected and dusted off all my old school reports which made some very interesting reading. As an example of one subject report that ultimately changed my life, my Chemistry teacher rightly wrote I could never consider Medicine with my present grades. However, it inspired me to raise my grade E in the mock exams to grade A in the real exam (just what the Doctor ordered!) Essentially I really thought 'fxxx you' but that F word was still on the forbidden list and not publicly used until The Sex Pistols infamously were encouraged and happy to do so multiple times on live television in December 1976. It caused a national sensation and in my opinion still is a most infamous and wicked piece of vintage television. As for my chemistry teacher, I can really only be grateful to him for lighting the fire I needed to succeed.

So to life.

I have always appreciated and been grateful for my life. However, of all our friends, two have stood out and wowed me. Yet ironically it is these two who, in the last few months and weeks, have both caused me to seriously reflect on the meaning of life.

Jon was a computer genius, had made his fortune, had a lovely wife and family with three super sons, was greatly respected and enjoying the fruits of his career. He had an amazing collection of working computers, so much so that he had even set up a working museum open to the public and for school outings. He would always be the perfect host, and showered his enthusiasm and knowledge whilst giving a fascinating history on the development of computers.

Apart from his family and enjoying life to the full (including drinking wine raised from the Titanic, and yes, it was awful!) his other life passion was mountaineering. He had twice tried to climb Everest, but on both occasions was thwarted by both the avalanche in 2014 and by the 2015 earthquake in Nepal, which claimed over three thousand lives. Fortunately, he was essentially in the right place at both times, although witnessing the avalanches he was never able to find out whether a party of Koreans they passed in 2015 survived or not.

Just months ago in preparation for another assault on Everest he was climbing another one of the tallest Mountains in the world at Shishapangma in the Himalayas.

On this particular climb he was in the leading group of three, all tied together. They decided to stop to let the other seven of the group catch up. Tragically, unbeknown to them and impossible to detect, they sat down on a snow bridge which collapsed underneath them. Jon was the first to fall into the crevice followed by his two colleagues. He fell twenty five metres into a wide crevice and another ten metres into a narrow one. The leader of the whole expedition was also involved and was the sole survivor of the three. Despite his initial concussion and injuries he was able to be rescued and he could confirm that he had seen the other two bodies. It has since been impossible to reach Jon to retrieve his body, so he is now hanging by his haversack for time immemorial in an ice crevice.

Stephen, another great friend I admired is a renowned medical specialist as well as owning a winery, and some top restaurants. He too has a great zest for life, a fantastic wife and three great children. He is a dedicated father and the family have shared the most fabulous holidays. He is also the most generous of souls, always lavishly entertaining and donating his time despite his busy work schedule. It was only two days ago that his wife informed us that he has pancreatic cancer. We can only hope for the best as he enters a tortuous journey of surgery and chemotherapy which we will endeavour to support as best as we can.

All three of these events have left fresh wounds.

So life – what's its meaning?

It's a precious gift and can end at any time. People cling to it when it is almost gone, instead of making the most of it, in the fullness of every day.

I have a simple philosophy which works for me - and if I could only pass on one piece of life advice to my grandchildren this would be it:

What is the Meaning of life? A life of Meaning.

What is a life of Meaning? A life of Purpose

What is a life of Purpose? A life of Service.

This certainly fits my career in the medical profession, which I will elaborate on.

Better business

I certainly believe in a work smart play hard philosophy, and aim to make every consultation of value to create a positive empowerment for my patients.

Two years ago myself and my practice nurse (and diabetic educator) attended an eighteen-month course on diabetes run by the Australian government. Diabetes is becoming the world's number one epidemic with 1.2 million cases in Australia alone, and projections of up to 2 million in the future. Although Australia has arguably one of the best health services in the world, we were astonished at the results across the country. Only 35% of patients with diabetes had good control as indicated by an HBA1c of 7 or below (HBA1c is a long-term marker of three months' average blood sugar control).

We had been working at the coal face of general practice and, although pleased that our health clinic recorded results at '71% good control' which were categorised as 'outstanding', we were concerned at the poor results across the country. It got us thinking that we were obviously doing something beyond other practices.

On further research I was staggered that so many GPs do not treat diabetes aggressively until it is already well established. In fact there are over 500,000 diabetic patients in Australia stuck on just the basic diabetes medication, Metformin, when there are so many other options and therapies that can be added to improve control. In my opinion the management of diabetes can clearly be improved by better education both of patients and even the medical profession itself.

I also believe there is a strong correlation between the belief and inspiration of a medical practitioner and clinical outcomes. In inspiring and empowering patients, if medical practitioners aren't empowered then neither will their patients be.

It has been shown that treating diabetes early and keeping it under control from day one has massive long term health benefits and vastly reduced health complications

With our success and statistics in diabetes management we have established the foundations to help advise and plan health policies. In fact, at times I feel that I have needed to become a de facto health minister, with several published articles in the medical press being presented to the Health Minister Susan Lay, and also having many ideas mirrored by The Royal Australian College of General Practitioners (RACGP).

Without going into detail we have really pushed the idea of both 'The Medical Home,' i.e. continuing health care from essentially one nominated GP within a practice and their team support of allied health workers for better and sustainable health outcomes, and the benefits of health assessments and care plans for chronic health conditions. Presently my ideas include introducing accountability, such as outcome payments for GPs on reaching health goals. This is still an evolving work in action, and yet it is gratifying to see that it is possible to trace some of the government's health policies to my original articles and research. The RACGP were even more positive, stating that Australia could lead the world in health care.

With our proven coalface statistics in diabetes we have the recipe to make a bigger impact on the world. Although one-on-one patient care has obviously worked for us to empower our patients, to help make 'The World A Better Place,' we need to create an online programme. My team have already enthusiastically thrown their support into setting up an online diabetes programme and we are obtaining great original research from several drug companies and innovative nutritional advice from highly respected Australian institutions such as the Baker IDI Heart and Diabetes Institute and top ranking Australian universities.

It's interesting to reflect over the last few years. Certainly six years ago we had little idea how to impact the world, so philanthropy via the Buy1Give1 ('B1G1') giving engine and movement has opened the door, and we have witnessed the effects of regular donations making small ripples to change the world. My wife Helen has been a passionate supporter of B1G1, finding that it gave her business a true heart. With such a privileged wealth of inspiration, which we are so appreciative and grateful for, we have tried to create even greater waves ourselves.

In addition to actively recruiting other members to the B1G1 philosophy, Helen has also been asked to make speeches about businesses 'that give' including at 'The Telstra Business Awards' and 'Women in Business Awards'. We have also been privileged to walk the walk and talk the talk with visits to Borneo, Bali, Cambodia & India, witnessing how well the organisations that B1G1 support enhance the world.

And in an even shorter timeframe, it was only two years ago that we attended the government APCC course on diabetes. At that time I would never have dreamt that, because of that course, I would become so involved in diabetes and medical health policies.

So if I could pass only one piece of business advice to my grandchildren, it would be:

If you have passion and a belief that you can make a positive change about making your community and the world a better place, then take up the challenge. As Masami Sato (the founder of Buy1Give1) says, in her

Giving Business book, 'create the maximum impact in a meaning-driven world', after all, the meaning of life is a meaning of purpose and service.

Footnote 1. *I have been informed by Sue, (Jon's wife) that the Korean mountaineers all survived.*

Footnote 2. *Best excuse ever not to immediately reply to an email. I emailed my cousin Nicholas re more information about his work with the orangutans and pygmy elephants. To quote his reply: 'Will be jumping off a building in a moment but can do it in a sec - sent on iPhone'*

Avoid the action vortex

Based in Australia, Heather is:

- Founder and Director of The Elevation Company, providing Values Based Leadership consultancy and support to businesses, groups and individuals throughout Australasia.
- Founder and Director of Green SuperCamp Australia, offering personal leadership, academic acceleration and environmental awareness programmes for young people.
- Winner of the Most Trusted Business Leader Award in the Australian Trust Awards 2015.
- Co-author of the 'Millionaire Coach' book, offering insights into building abundance and wealth.
- A Content Specialist for The Growth Project, providing leadership development for emerging Australian charities.
- A strong believer that all any of us really wants in this life is to love and be loved and be known, loved and 'got' for who we truly are!

Here is the advice she would give to her grandchildren...

Better business

Everything in business must begin with understanding why – why am I doing this, why does it matter, why do I want to have this impact in the world?

Yet, in many cases we get busy asking ourselves 'how' we change things. This is usually borne out of difficulties or challenges. But asking the 'how' question simply increases the size and perception of the scarcity or lack that prompted the question in the first place.

In order to create change, we then decide to take some action, any action, to increase the possibility of a better outcome. This then leads to increases in motivation, which in turn, adds to us taking more action. The challenge comes when we simply increase the 'how' generated action and motivation, without objective reflection on the value of the action, which effectively has us sucked into the Action Vortex! In a business, as in life, this leads to lots of action, but often with very limited results.

By contrast, if we ask ourselves the 'WHY' question, we are more likely to connect to what inspires us, what 'calls to us' and therefore what puts us into greater flow.

When we are inspired and inspiring, we get into a state of attraction, which leads to greater inspiration and in turn, creates even greater attraction. At this end of the spectrum, our actions are far more powerful and our leadership attracts people and opportunities that build our success and increase the positive impact we can make in our business and the world.

It is important to understand the WHY behind what we are doing, as this sets the framework for our higher purpose and is at the core of all we do. Your 'Big Why' gives you clarity about the essential energy that must be in all things for you to be successful, content and in 'flow'.

Knowing your own 'why' and the 'why' of each of your team members, will ensure you access the greatest sense of flow in the work you do, which in turn, adds to the development of a positive business culture and a sense of shared purpose for you, your team and those you serve. The 'why' behind what you are doing usually reflects your values.

Values are the principles or standards by which we live and work.

They are fundamentally important to us in that they influence our actions and choices and drive what we do and how we do it. It is also fair to say the way we understand ourselves and the world is viewed through the 'filter' of our values and therefore, they inform the way we create meaning from our experiences.

Our values help us to determine whether our actions are right or wrong, effective or ineffective, and this same filtering process is applied to all aspects of our business and life.

Our values will also inform the way we judge other people's actions as good or bad, right or wrong, helpful or unhelpful and so it is essential that you understand what your values are.

And our values can change according to our experience and context, so you should review them regularly to ensure they support you - your work, relationships and understanding of yourself.

Creating a business that is in alignment with your highest values will increase your effectiveness and success. Knowing the values of your team members and braiding this with the values of the business will also add to your effectiveness and is a cornerstone of strong leadership.

In this context, leadership is the ability to understand people and inspire them to work toward an agreed and mutually enrolling vision or goal, the benefits of which are felt by those we serve, the members of the team and the broader business. Management is more focussed on the administration, systems and processes that ensure accountability and quality control.

Therefore, it is the work of the true leader that creates inspiration.

And these are some of the keys to great leadership:

Why - Strong leaders know the WHY behind what they do, and understand the importance of knowing the WHY of each member of their team. They also know that being able to enrol and feed into each team member's BIG WHY and braid this with the organization's WHY is crucial to team cohesion and individual satisfaction and achievement.

Certainty - Great leaders possess a confidence and clarity, borne of self-awareness. Furthermore, this certainty is contagious. Team members are naturally drawn to them, seek their advice, and feel more confident as a result. When challenged, they remain open to new ideas and perspectives. They are confident that their ideas, opinions and choices are well-informed and reflect the collective view, because they know their people! Strong leaders may make mistakes, but when this is discovered, they take responsibility, look to the opportunity for shared learning and act to change things quickly.

Growth - Extraordinary leaders focus on the growth and development of their team. This means they learn the best ways to acknowledge, support, encourage and challenge each member, to ensure the highest possible level of engagement. The development of a culture of learning is essential and a powerful leader will create and hold a supportive environment, where people feel able to share their mistakes in the interests of shared learning and growth.

Accountability - Extraordinary leaders take responsibility for everyone's performance, especially their own. They have strong capacity for insightfulness and will check in with themselves to see what the learning is in any situation, and what (if anything) they can do to provide stronger leadership in the future. From this place, they will then look outward to ensure the accountability of others. This creates a culture of personal responsibility that allows team members to hold each other more accountable.

Communication – True leaders recognise that effective communication begins with listening. The capacity to ask great questions and explore unvisited aspects of the thoughts, feelings and inspirations of team members, is evident in strong leaders. They also have the ability to 'listen beyond the words' to discover the values, beliefs and inspirations of their team. Speaking into the 'listening' of each person increases understanding and cohesion and builds trust. Recognising the patterns of interaction between team members, and ensuring these are positive and growth promoting, is also at the forefront of the contribution of an extraordinary leader.

Optimism - True leaders are a source of positive and persistent energy, often borne of the knowledge that they are doing what they were born to do. They generally communicate easily and in a manner that inspires. They operate from an open-hearted place and are genuinely interested in other people's welfare and growth. They seem wired to create solutions and always know what to say to inspire, uplift or reassure. Importantly, they also know the difference between motivating team members (a force from behind) and inspiring them (a force from in front) to reach for greater outcomes.

Transparency - Strong leaders treat others the way they wish to be treated and avoid hiding things, even those of a personal nature. They are extremely ethical and believe that honesty, integrity and transparency form the foundation of success. They know and embody their own and the organisation's values, such that employees are inspired by their example of how to live by their highest values. They share information openly and enroll team members in decision-making whenever possible. If required, they are also able to make decisions that may not be popular, but provide a clear context for why the decision was made that way.

Focus - Great leaders recognise the importance of planning ahead and the value of being well organised. They explore multiple scenarios and the possible impacts of their decisions, while considering viable alternatives and consulting with appropriate people. They then make plans that create the greatest possible success for all concerned. They then create clear strategies, systems and processes to ensure high performance is tangible, easily defined, and monitored. And they communicate their plans effectively to ensure maximum enrolment of team members in achieving goals.

Inspiration – Powerful leaders are clear about what inspires them and stay connected to this. They articulate their highest values and are clear about how to live in accordance with them. They know themselves well and value the practice of self-reflection and life-long learning. They communicate clearly, concisely, and consistently and in a manner that inspires everyone to be and give their best to mutual benefit. They challenge their people by setting high and attainable standards and expectations – modelled by their own behavior - and then give the support, tools, training, scope and autonomy to pursue those goals and become the best employees they can possibly be, so they feel a greater sense of achievement and success, the organisation grows and those they serve feel and sense a genuine difference.

Inspirational leaders recognise that the greatest outcomes for all concerned are borne out of braiding individual endeavor with organisational endeavor – and serving the unique needs, wants and inspirations of those to whom they provide service.

Better life

There is something in each and every one of us that calls us to create a life of inspiration, to dream big and walk powerfully toward that dream, to make the difference we were born to make – even just to live a life less ordinary seems a given.

We are born with a natural capacity for, and focus on, love and the world is a rich tapestry of possibility, enchantment, creativity, imagination, learning and magic. It's as if there's a homing signal inside each and every one of us that calls us toward a full and evolving sense of who we really are at our essence; the discovery of our own unique truth and the fullest expression of that truth with those we love and the world around us.

Then, one day we realise we have lost contact with that calling, that inner knowing and possibly even the sense of our truth altogether.

So, what the hell happened?

Where did all our dreams go, when did we stop drinking beautiful wine, walking on beaches and sharing our thoughts and feelings with others well into the tiny hours of the day? What happened to the quest to know our own heart and the heart and soul of others as well as we know the road to and from work or the children's school gate? When did we stop BEING and start DOING and let that way of life become so much the norm, that when we meet someone who's heart is wide open, we either find it startlingly attractive or a little annoying?

These are questions we all need to face on this beautiful, inspired and disturbing journey we call life.

The difficulty begins when we allow ourselves to be sucked in to the 'vortex of action' and take up residence there, such that we don't even realise we have lost the sense of possibility, let go of our dreams, disconnected from the people we love, squashed our sense of wonder and magic, and lost contact with the essence of who we truly are.

Then, little by little, our activity levels and the consequent pace of life, creeps up and up, until going flat out becomes normal. It certainly was in my family and community, all of whom were unwitting victims of 'creepage'. This is the insidious force that paves the way, indeed courts and seduces us, into the sticky trap of the action vortex, where the art and joy of simply being seem beyond our reach, even if we are conscious enough to know we have lost it.

We have been taught to value certain things, to think and feel certain things, to strive to achieve certain things by which our family, community, profession, religion or culture define success. Yet, if you sit at the bedside of a dying friend, rarely will you hear them express regret that they didn't buy that house on the water, drive that Ferrari, work longer hours or take the promotion. If there is regret, it will be about the amount of times they didn't say I love you to the people nearest, the hours they didn't come home early from work, the energy that went into the business or promotion and not into family, the inner journey that never received adequate attention, the time not spent with children, and so on. Meaning doesn't lie in things or material possessions – it lies within us and within our relationships!

It is my firm belief that all any of us really wants in this life is to love and be loved and to be known, loved and 'got' for who we truly are. In the final hour, little else matters!

So, no matter who you might feel has authored or influenced your journey, you have choices – indeed you've been making them all along. Consciously or otherwise, YOU have actually authored your life to this point, no matter how much you may wish to point the finger at someone else!

That realisation can feel like a bitter pill....AND the road to freedom all rolled into one!

You may not want to take full responsibility for the life you are currently living, but let's face it, something in you made you pick up this book – and you have read through to this point!

So, maybe the still, small voice inside you that knows there's MORE TO LIFE is still there and is patiently (or desperately) urging you to sit up and pay attention. The challenge is to know how to change things so you can once again rediscover the truth of who you are and live into all you were born to be. It is knowledge of the SELF that has the greatest bearing on an abundant, fulfilling and meaningful life.

If there's one thing I recommend as a central and fundamental life lesson it is this...

KNOW THYSELF!

Invest in discovering the truth of who you are and share it boldly with the world.

Find the difference you were born to make and give your whole heart into the service of that difference, so you can impact the greatest number of lives in the most sustainable way and leave your true legacy.

Better world

We live in a culture that greatly values knowledge as a means by which to solve problems. It has been demonstrated many times, for instance, that the best way to assist people to move out of poverty is to provide knowledge, to educate.

Then, at some stage in the development of our culture, we came to value action.

Thomas H. Huxley once said: 'The great end of life is not knowledge but action.' This has been extrapolated to a widely used expression that 'knowledge is not knowledge until it is turned into action'. So, we set out on our path to find knowledge and then apply it, such that it braids through our action and increases our motivation– the knowledge comes to life through action and the action builds our motivation.

When the action we take enables us to achieve more and we begin to build a sense of momentum, we are more motivated, we learn more and we are then enthusiastic about taking greater action. This creates a cycle where knowledge applied becomes action... and then in turn, the action creates greater success and learning, which motivates us and feeds the knowledge... which then generates more action. So, the cycle looks like this:

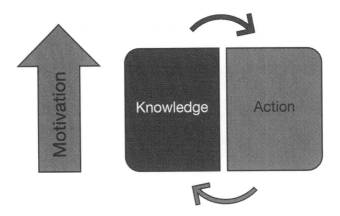

This can be a very effective way to create movement and generate change. And, indeed, this principle is at the heart of a great deal of teaching in so many aspects of our lives, from the education of our children, through business development and change management, to popular diets and personal growth.

If you stop and think about it, it's a core principle at the heart of so many different aspects of our lives.

My concern is this motivation is a form of movement AWAY FROM, so this is effectively 'problem solving' thinking. At the heart of this way of being (or should I say DOING!) is problem thinking. Now granted, we all have a few problems to solve, so you may be wondering why you feel like there's a 'but' coming.

Let me be clear that this is not a principle I think is fundamentally flawed.

However, somewhere along the way we become so focused on and fascinated by our ability to gain knowledge, take action and increase motivation that we work ourselves into a frenzy of gathering knowledge and taking action in order to increase motivation and eventually we enter into what I call the **Action Vortex**.

This is the beginning of the 'hamster on the treadmill' syndrome.

We gain knowledge and apply it to action – when that works, our increased motivation has us simply 'rinse and repeat' until we are captured by our own Action Vortex. Once we enter this Action Vortex, it becomes increasingly difficult to see how we can possibly do things differently and so we simply keep on with generating more action.

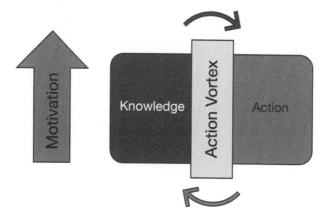

How many times can you recall talking about how busy you are and how much there is to do and how you never seem to have time for things you once enjoyed or loved and how you're always on the go and there's not enough hours in the day and how quickly the year is flying by... and so on?

This is the 'talk' of someone caught in the Action Vortex. This is also the 'talk' of an entire society caught in the Action Vortex.

We are working longer hours than ever before - and still can't get ahead. We have a huge array of supposedly time saving household appliances and office equipment - and we still run out of time. The fact that we all seem to be doing it doesn't make it right, useful or central to the development, let alone the elevation, of the human experience.

So, what's the alternative?

Imagine a continuum which at one end is all about KNOWLEDGE, ACTION and MOTIVATION – problem thinking – and at the other end is all about WISDOM, ATTRACTION and INSPIRATION – creative thinking. Let me explain.

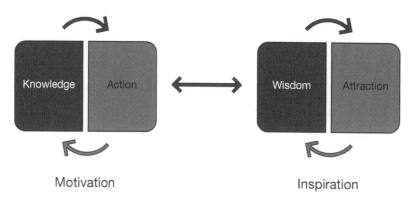

In this context, knowledge generally comes from an outside source, whilst wisdom is a form of inner understanding. While both are valuable and have their place, by far the more powerful is to be in a state of INSPIRATION. At this end of the continuum, there is a strength of understanding of one's own inner truth and wisdom – a sense of certainty about who we are and what we stand for. This then generates a level of congruence and energetic resonance that creates ATTRACTION to other people, opportunities and experiences.

The greater the wisdom, the stronger the attraction, and the more the attraction, the more certain and powerful the wisdom...and so the cycle goes generating INSPIRATION, which is a force TOWARD. The force toward which we are drawn through inspiration is LOVE, the elevation of the human experience! The more inspired we are, the more connected and loving we feel - to ourselves, each other and the world around us.

We have all met people on our journey who seem to be really 'lucky', in that good things just seem to come to them and all the right people and opportunities seem to just fall at their feet. That's not LUCK, unless we create our own luck! That's ATTRACTION!

When people sense our wisdom (inner knowing and certainty) and see our attraction, they too become more inspired.

So, find your place of balance on the Action/Attraction continuum and create a life fashioned by inspiration, attraction and service. You were born to make a difference in this world and the greater the inspiration and 'flow' you experience, the greater the legacy you leave.

From little things big things grow

Based in Australia, Helen:

- Is the owner of Knox Audiology, a hearing diagnostic business in Melbourne, that has expanded to four centres in just 8 years
- Has worn many hats, including deputy director of nursing, business advisor and health counsellor using her training in behaviour therapy and clinical hypnosis
- Managed a medical practice that won a major Australian award for its health education and patient care
- A passionate advocate of corporate social responsibility and the 'power of small'
- Married with three adult children

Here is the advice she would give to her grandchildren...

Better business

'How to run a business is very similar to playing netball. Each person has a clear position (e.g. goal attack, wing defence), a clearly defined scope for their role (what they can do and where they can go), and those roles are matched to the person's strengths (you need to be able shoot if you are a goal shooter).

Winning at netball, and in business, needs more than that. It needs a clear goal that everyone is committed to and accepts (to win the premiership), a defined strategy that is easy to execute (step 1, 2, 3), and continuous practice of core strengths and of that winning strategy. So, if you're a shooter, practice your shooting. If you're a defender, practice defending. Then, as a team, routinely practice your winning plan and execution steps so that when it comes to 'game time' you simply implement to win without having to think too much about it.'

Yolanda Gerge
Director of Identity Consulting - a specialist consultancy devoted to realising the potential and growth of private practices

'Dring dring... dring dring.'

The phone echoed loudly amongst the walls of our box like Saundersfoot home. A home wherein the windows would rattle with the winds, and out in the garden Fred, our pet tortoise, would freely roam. My grandad, my mum and I stood in eager anticipation. It was almost as though I could already tell, this moment could influence the rest of my life. My mother, donning her favourite floral dark green 1960's dress, picked up the large black receiver and placed it to her pearl ear-ringed ear.

We all leaned forward, hearing those crackles, then the telephonist stating that she would be connecting the call, then those long distance pips. Finally we heard Nanna say 'Hello'. The hairs on my arms stood on end. Was that really her voice, calling from 10,700 miles away as the crow flies in the Antipodes?

In that instant my five-year-old mind was captivated. We can now hear someone, and connect to them, no matter how far away they are on the other side of the globe. It felt as if we are really always connected.

When Nanna returned from Australia and gave me a koala toy with an odd pouch, I conjured up a sweeping image of what it must be like on the other side of the world; the colour of the sea and sky, the warm air. Perhaps in this moment I knew that one day, I too was going to visit. Even now, that unbridled eruption of joy within me bubbles away at those thoughts.

Years later, now living in Australia, my career in health provided me with the avenue of world adventure I had yearned for since receiving that phone call. This drive pushed me to see the world, to bond with people from faraway countries, and to pursue that burning desire for connection which I believe radiates such joy in us all. I embraced an inquisitiveness for active listening, to truly connect authentically with others. That is, listening not only to the words, but also between the words. It has been integral in my mission in life to spread the joy of authentic connection which is a valuable asset to raising a family, and also for running a business.

My studies have taught me to appreciate the importance of connection to our world which formed the foundation for us to purchase a diagnostic hearing centre in 2007. This supported my passion for keeping people connected in the world - really connected with their senses and hoping they too could feel the presence using their senses that I had felt on my travels.

However after the initial excitement, it started to become soul destroying, energy sapping work and I lost clarity and balance in the mayhem and frustration of a growing business as my role and the roles of others were not clearly defined.

With marketing, websites, contracts, IT, money, I was on the steep learning curve of the business world. We knew what to do, but how? All the staff appeared to be working hard, but there was a lack of ease and flow. Over the following 18 months, just like on a netball team, we analysed the strengths and weaknesses of all the staff, put systems in place to collect data and restructured the business.

However, I remained feeling uncomfortable with the necessity to focus on money. I was questioning the greater business purpose.

Six months later I received an email to hear a speaker in the city that realised my reason why I participated in business. That night I met Paul Dunn, an inspirational speaker who talked about connection and creating a greater meaning in business than money. Yes, putting a heart in business. This just felt right and at the end of the talk going against my normal checking and cross referencing I signed up to an organisation - Buy1Give1: Business for Good - and it changed business for me overnight. Even on the toughest of days, knowing we were making a difference in the world at large was a powerful incentive to keep going. *'Ears That Keep Giving'* was created! This is an expression we use for the fact that every time we see a patient there is an automatic giving to a social enterprise around the world.

Giving has put the 'Why' back into our business, and with everybody in the team having a clearly defined scope for their role, we share a reason to come to work every day to bring our business to even greater heights knowing we are making a positive difference around the world.

Could the reality be that when people give, they reinforce and connect to their purpose? Our business shares the inspiration with our team members, suppliers, clients and customers; we intend to give hope, joy and a smile to someone else from across the world just like I felt was possible as that five year old child!

Better life

An old Cherokee is telling his granddaughter about a fight that is going on inside himself. He said it is between two wolves. One is evil: anger, envy, sorrow, regret, greed, arrogance, self-pity, guilt, resentment, inferiority, lies, false pride, superiority and ego. The other is good: joy, peace, love, hope, serenity, humility, kindness, benevolence, empathy, generosity, truth, compassion and faith. The granddaughter thought about it for a minute and then asked her grandfather, 'Which wolf wins?'

The old Cherokee simply replied, 'The one I feed.'

'I woke as the car flew through the air. It stopped half embedded in a flurry of sand. The whirring engine slowed to a stop and an eerie stillness filled the hot arid air. I gently pulled at my leg trapped between the front seats and crawled through the shattered side window. I stood up, surrounded by a sea of sand, in the middle of Death Valley, Nevada, and then I collapsed.'

The year before had been an intense period of adventurous travel. I had been backpacking all around the world. This experience seemed to have heightened my senses and somehow seemed to slow time.

First stop was Bangkok where the spiciness of the food ignited in me more than just my taste buds. The vibrant colours and the unfamiliar sounds filled my mind, I breathed in to the exotic smells that wafted through the air announcing to me the arrival of a tropical country. Each moment was like a picture frame which I felt would be embedded in me forever. Tuning into my senses I felt so alive, each day seeming like a lifetime. This 'presence' (I now know it to be) stayed with me throughout my travels.

'Yet I now stare up at the twinkling mass of stars in the pitch black sky above me. I had no choice, my head and body were stuck firmly down to a hard board, pain surging through my body. I looked up at the paramedic to the left of my head and heard her repetitively say that my breathing was too quick and that I needed to slow it down. Start counting, she had said, counting out loud counting each breath and to breathe - yes, breathe - deeply into my belly. Everything felt so disorientated and confusing, but I found myself putting my attention on my breath. Slowly, very slowly, I began to breathe more and more deeply and then from somewhere I felt a wave of acceptance wash over me, accepting all the foibles of myself as a human being, letting go of the pain and I began to just focus on those twinkling delights in the sky through the helicopter window above me. In each frame by frame moment my world slowed to an incredible clarity of thought. I felt unconditional acceptance of what is. I was present, no emotion, as I gently let go of all I thought my life was to be and opened to the possibilities of the unknown.'

The Las Vegas hospital doctor could not have appreciated the magnitude of the words that he spoke. 'Yes, you have two spinal fractures, but you will walk.'

I had already accepted I was to live a very different life, perhaps to never walk again. I know I could have managed, I know that with my determination I could have still lived a rich and rewarding life, but now I was open to recreate my future with a newfound enthusiasm, gratitude and energy that was greater than I had ever felt before. I again breathed into this moment, felt my fear drift away to nothing. I was free. From that day on I felt connected to my own body's inner wisdom and knew how to live from my heart rather than my chatterbox mind. As I look back now I have been learning to dance with this 'essence' throughout my life.

Years later during a conference, I was asked what adversity I had experienced in my lifetime from which I could learn and have gratitude for that event. Amazingly, on reflection, I am surprised to notice I did not recall this past event, which I now put down to my total acceptance by being present to myself that may have otherwise caused me to feed an emotion like resentment, self-pity, guilt etc.

I know that every morning when I wake, open the curtains and see the sky I am filled with excitement and an energetic spark for life. I deeply appreciate the gift of a loving family, friends, a truly rewarding business and the tenacity I have to live each day with enthusiasm. In effect this past event has caused me to listen to my heart, quieten my mind and to choose to make a positive difference every day with others to the world.

That was an extreme experience which I have recounted but it has a powerful message I'd like to share.

Whenever adversity strikes, turn to your breath, consciously breathe deeply and take time to repetitively move eyes down as you accept everything as it is and to look up above you as you create a new vision, it may sound crazy but a great acceptance of life lies here.

'Let it go.
Let it out.
Let it all unravel.
Let it free and it can be
A path on which to travel.'

Michael Leunig

Better world

'Never doubt that a small group of thoughtful, committed citizens can change the world; indeed, it's the only thing that ever has.'
Margaret Mead

Connecting a small Melbourne business to the world, I believe that being small doesn't mean you can't make a difference, and I am thrilled to be a partner in the global giving initiative known as Buy1GIVE1.

It's a fantastic way to give back that is both simple and powerful.

When someone does business with us, it automatically makes a difference to the lives of others in our world. When a private hearing aid is sold to a patient in Melbourne, a goat is automatically given to a family in Odede, Kenya to provide a sustainable income. Medication, water and food supplies are some of the other ways we support families.

The fun thing is, we now measure, and get excited about, the number of goats we donate, rather than the number of patients we see.

In furthering this newfound drive, I have pursued possibly my most colourful and exciting adventures to date. I have travelled to new places with groups of like-minded small business owners from around the world. These B1G1 study tours have enabled me to walk my talk, connecting me first hand with so many caring organisations and NGOs.

For example we have witnessed the tragic devastation in Borneo of the palm oil plantations denuding the forest, causing many endangered species such as the critically endangered Borneo orangutans and Borneo pygmy elephants, to lose their precious habitat. But the lungs of the world suffer as well. The soil is so poor that the palm plantations are unsustainable – and eventually, after the plantation dies, the residual soil is nutrient exhausted, and nothing can grow. To me, this was insanity.

While visiting these plantations we spent a day planting numerous trees in a bid to make a small difference now that would one day grow to help the environment. With the John Fawcett Foundation, we visited local Balinese villages to experience their profound but simple ways of giving back hope in the areas of sight restoration and blindness. It was a fantastic example as to how the gift of glasses or the restoration of sight after cataract surgery could make such a dramatic difference to the individual, their family and their community. By witnessing their heartfelt appreciation I shared the delight of being there for another. It felt like a magical experience.

This power of small can be seen in countless situations across the world. In Siem Reap, Cambodia, we visited the NGO 'This Life', which runs the 'Pedaling out of Poverty' project which provides a second-hand bicycle and lock to each student. This simple means of transportation gives the student an ability to attend secondary school and continue his or her education, breaking the cycle of poverty. We also built playgrounds at primary schools to encourage more pupils to attend and feed through the system in which many Cambodian children take 10 years or more to complete primary school due to being held back consistently. Overall, more than half of Cambodian schoolchildren do not complete primary school at all.

In Mumbai I was staggered at the power of small.

In one kitchen we saw how 65,000 hot healthy meals are prepared for local schools every day. We also witnessed the Dabbawala lunch box deliveries across Mumbai. They are efficient and on time with a high level of service, a low-cost and a simple operating system. The Dabbawala's success is proof that with the right system in place, ordinary workers can achieve extraordinary results.

I knew our giving was supporting others by creating a hand up to our world. Now connecting in person on my travels, I was taken aback by the immense gratitude that struck me and filled me with such a joy that seemed to permeate and travel back to everyone in our giving community in Melbourne. Could this be the authentic contentment and happiness we all desire?

Freya our audiologist says 'The charity work our business is involved in is a big part of why I chose to join the team. It is fantastic to know that not only am I helping people directly in the clinic, but also all around the world.'

And I believe that the impact we each have on the world is greater than we could ever imagine and the choices we make every day have far-reaching consequences. We like to see people get connected, and done compassionately, running a business with a social conscience helps us to express our 'soul' purpose!

The ripple effect of one small business when connected to other like-minded businesses around the globe can truly make a positive difference and spread waves of kindness that will flow all over the world.

Together we can make 7.4 billion differences a day

Based in the UK, Jane is:

- Owner of a fast-growing bookkeeping company
- Mentor to bookkeepers on value pricing and business development
- Featured in the book 'A Practical Approach to Value Pricing'
- Contributor to the book 'How to Build a Better Bookkeeping Practice'
- Author of several articles for the accounting profession, and
- A true believer in the awesome power in data, huge advocate of the 'accounting revolution' and a die-hard optimist

Here is the advice she would give to her grandchildren...

Better business

Choose your inspiration wisely.

I decided to start a business for all of the wrong reasons. I didn't know they were the wrong reasons. They seemed big and important and noble and reasonable at the time. I'm an intelligent, capable person and I am very good at my chosen vocation - so starting a business made sense, right?

No. It didn't.

Now, I can't even remember what those reasons were - and for a very long time, I was simply drifting through my business, earning a living and getting through each day, week, month.

What I really needed was inspiration. Life was dull, business was unsatisfactory and my achievements were devoid of pleasure. There was no 'WOW!'

I needed to open my mind to the possibilities that were out there - think outside the box and have goals, a strategy and a plan. Take risks. Have a reason for being in business that was bigger and brighter and bolder than anything that, at that time, I could imagine.

I didn't have any of those things.

I was in a bubble. A bubble of work and need and money and clients. I never looked up, I never looked out and I never thought I could be on the same stage as those most admired and revered leaders - some of whom have contributed to this book... with me.

Suddenly I decided to go out and find people I admired, and I got out there and shared their space. I went to the conferences they were speaking at and enrolled on the courses that they taught and joined the organisations that they supported. And my mind was opened to a whole new way of thinking about business, about success, about what I could do to be successful and what I could do to make that mean something.

So my pearl of wisdom is that you should go out of your way to meet the people who are outside of your comfort zone and surround yourself with inspirational people who have new and different experiences to share with you. Learn from them and integrate into new circles.

You will go further and have more impact on your world if you broaden your horizons. And you can only do that when you let go of your ego and your perceived inadequacies and embrace new experiences.

Be prepared to be humble. But remember always that you are not inferior to, only less experienced than, the great leaders around you. The sooner you move in these circles, the sooner you will belong in them.

Get yourself a higher purpose. Make sure you are focused on a goal that the people you surround yourself with can relate to - something that will create a culture, a tribe, accountability and a shared drive to achieve something bigger, better and brighter than you can ever hope to achieve alone.

Suddenly, being in business will have meaning, purpose and joy.

Find a purpose, embrace inspiration, and most of all, believe in your ability to change the world.

Better life

I believe that most things in life are experienced very differently depending on what stage in life you are at when you do them and, in most cases, the experiences are no more or less profound, beautiful or life changing. But in different ways, and for different reasons.

In nearly all cases, the timing is about when it is right for you, rather than when you are the right age, or in the right space.

An exception to this is travelling the world.

I believe that you will never travel again like you will when you are young.

You will never experience the same freedom. You will never be more open to connecting with others, changing the plan (if you even have one to start with), going with the flow and immersing yourself in new experiences.

Being a grown-up is a marvellous thing and it comes with many opportunities not open to, or easy for, the young. However it also comes with responsibility, a reluctance to stray too far from the path, and less free time. While travel is still a privilege and should never be undervalued, it becomes about different things.

It is often about 'getting away' rather than 'going to', it's about shutting off from your normal world, rather than being open to new experiences, it's about relaxing and re-charging, rather than about being energised and inspired by something different. It's about comfort and reward, rather than making the most of what you have.

I honestly think that travel should be as normal a part of growing up as going to college or learning to drive. The wealth of experiences, new opportunities, and connections that you will gain doing this will be invaluable as you start your career. A year or two spent exploring our world will accelerate you in life, in business and in your relationships, not hold you back.

So pack a rucksack, grab your best friends, and travel as far as you can, experience as many things as possible and come home awakened, aware and ready to bring your experience to the table in your adult life.

Better world

Every single thing we do makes a difference. Every way in which we choose to act, every life that we touch, every sentence that is said has an impact.

Never assume that you are too small or too insignificant to make a difference and that, therefore, nothing that you do really matters. That is simply a denial of the responsibility you have in the world.

We are all accountable.

As Edmund Burke so memorably pointed out: *'All that is necessary for the triumph of evil is that good men do nothing.'*

Do not wait until you think the difference you can make is big enough to matter. Every single thing that you can do to make our world a better place makes our world a better place, and is therefore worth doing.

Do what you think is right. Stand by, and for, the things that you believe in.

If everybody alive today did one tiny thing every day to change our world, our world would change at a rate of 7.4 billion tiny things a day.

That's a BIG difference, every single day.

But if nobody took action until they felt they could do enough, nothing would ever be achieved.

To view the need in its entirety is too big and too daunting for most of us to comprehend – we shut off and we do nothing. Triumph in the tiny differences you make and know that enough tiny differences, made by enough individuals, have immense power to change the world.

The quality of your life is determined by the questions you ask

Based in Australia, Jeremy:

- Is an accountant who loves to support entrepreneurs to create, refine and exit their businesses in ways that fulfil their purpose and their goals.
- Has been passionate about working with businesses, mostly family businesses, for over twenty years.
- Is a partner at a leading accounting firm in Brisbane

Here is the advice he would give to his grandchildren...

Better business

You can have what seems to be a great idea, but without a customer you don't have a business.

You can follow your passion and do what you love, but without a customer you don't have a business.

Business starts with a customer. That doesn't necessarily mean 'the customer is always right'. Not every customer, anyway. Some can certainly be wrong.

But it starts with a customer - someone who has a problem that needs to be solved, or a desire to be fulfilled - and for whom you have an answer.

Once they have a customer, some business owners don't like to sell, especially those in businesses that are called professions. I believe that selling is educating, when done with integrity and authenticity, and with the needs of the customer held paramount. It is informing the customer about options available to them to solve their problem or fulfil their desire - to move them away from pain or towards pleasure.

How should integrity be measured? Is it black and white, zero and one - or is it a scale? If it's a scale, does it mean that if you do the right thing 9 times out of 10 you are doing well? I don't have an answer to these questions - but I do believe that if you reflect on them your understanding will grow.

Which reminds me, the quality of your life is enhanced by the quality of questions that you ask.

When it comes to business, both at the beginning and continuously throughout, ask 'Who is my customer?' and 'What do they most need or want right now?'

Most importantly, the best customer for a business will be one who believes in the true purpose for which the business exists – the 'why' of the business. And as Simon Sinek said, true purpose is always human. So it's important to understand and express the 'why' of a business.

Above all, realise that business is about relationships; and because of that, to be sustainable it is ultimately about trust.

Better life

One of the most challenging personal qualities to achieve in life, in my view, is to remove ego from decisions, relationships and achievements.

Letting go of ego in situations where it doesn't belong feels cleaner and simpler. When I finally got it, it came easily and naturally; it's such a good feeling.

Setting aside ego fosters peace within yourself, and with other people. It means not fretting over whether your idea gets chosen, or not saying 'I told you so'.

Removing ego from a relationship removes unhealthy competition and puts a focus on respect. Genuine love does not contain ego.

Letting go of ego is easier when you are relaxed, and when you accept that there is purpose in everything that happens in life.

Closely related to letting go of ego is the quality of humility. I believe that humility is one of the greatest traits to strive for in life. It is part of acknowledging that there is a greater power that provides us with the natural gifts we have been given. Humility allows space for the light to shine on others as well as on you.

Better world

Every person can make a positive impact in the world. And every positive impact, big or small, is worth making.

Some people have a single idea that makes a massive difference. That might be you.

If it is, be humble. And if it isn't, forget ego, and don't be dissuaded from finding the right way for you personally to be the change you wish to see in the world.

I believe that we are on this planet to interact, build community, and help each other.
We are most effective in making a difference when we work together, acknowledging each other's strengths.

Making the world a better place can only truly be done through relationships, working together for a cause. So again, always remember the place of humility and ego.

Build, learn, give and be true to who you are

Based in Australia, Kerrie is:

- An international speaker, award-winning leadership coach, author and life-long learner
- Passionate about traveling, meeting people, and inspiring a more connected and compassionate world
- Author of the books 'DO Talk To Strangers: How To Connect With Anyone, Anywhere', and 'Lifting The Lid on Quiet Achievers: Success Stories of Regional Entrepreneurs', along with seven co-authored titles
- Her family are her greatest inspiration, and she regards her calling to serve leaders and difference-makers as a joy

Here is the advice she would give to her grandchildren...

Better business

The key is to build teams, build community, build connection and build leadership.

You don't have to figure it all out on your own. Connect with others and learn from people of all ages. Build a team. Even if you're a solo-entrepreneur, you'll need others to be truly successful and make the difference you're capable of. You can do some amazing things on your own, and it's good to discover what you're capable of. It's even more incredible to build a team and create a bigger impact.

Connect with people who are different to you, in skill-set, natural gifting, and culture. Find common ground, shared vision, and celebrate diversity in ideas – you'll find creativity and innovation increases and delivers value, benefiting all around you.

The more you can build relationships with humility and authenticity, the more you'll find yourself and other people flourishing. We do our best when we can truly be ourselves, and let our inner light shine. It's a challenge to discover who we really are, and what we truly believe when we're surrounded and impacted by the influence of other people and culture. I'll continue on this theme in a little while. But in the meantime, let's take a closer look at leadership that BUILDS.

And, as you will see, the acronym for BUILDS is...

... Bold, Understanding, Insightful Leadership Delivers Success.

Bold – Be brave and take risks. You see the world differently to those around you. If you don't, please get out and travel more and talk to strangers. You take a risk when you share a new idea or when you ask a question no one else is asking – you'll often find that others wish they had the courage to. Your boldness will inspire others, and increase your confidence to keep stepping out. Sometimes this makes a small difference, sometimes you might wish you hadn't, but if your desire is to BUILD, all of the smaller moments of boldness will strengthen and prepare you for times you most need to speak up or take action, times when you can make a significant difference.

Understanding – Listen to people. Listen to yourself too. When you listen, take note of what you're listening for. Are you listening to hear that you're right, or are you listening with curiosity, to see how you can serve, and what you can learn? Can you be IN that moment, not bringing judgments or situations into the conversation, or fast-forwarding to what you'll say next, allowing insights to emerge, for both you and others? We tend to fill the gaps in conversation or allow others to fill the gaps. Practice by listening without interruption. Who has time for that you wonder? It's a valuable exercise, so please give it a go. Find a talkative child and ask them to explain their favourite thing to you.

Listening to someone, really listening, not only assures them that they matter, but also provides you with an opportunity to understand another perspective at a deeper level. Learn to ask questions that deepen their learning; questions that help them have insights which increases their own understanding of what matters to them and why. You will make a lasting impact. Not only will you have served them, but all who they serve. Understanding is not just about your understanding of what someone shares, but deepening theirs.

Insightful – Business is an amazing opportunity for personal growth if you're willing to face yourself, learn and grow. Take time to search out insights. Look at everyday situations with questions like 'what can I learn here?' Ask yourself questions, hire a coach to ask you what no one else will, and be OK with the awkward silence that may be there before the insight comes. Be OK with awkward – maybe even comfortable. Laugh every day. Humour and lightness pave the way to creativity, collaboration, insight and innovation. Laughter is indeed the best medicine.

Leadership – Study leadership, reflect on your experiences with leadership in your life, and ask others. Ask 'what works?' and focus on the strengths of leadership. If your focus is to 'not be like' a previous boss or leader, you're short-changing yourself (and others), and limiting your capacity to grow. Instead, focus on what you do want, rather than dwelling on someone else's negative attributes. Learn about the strengths of leaders, and discover your own strengths. How can you inspire others? Inspiring people is often something that great leaders aren't focused on doing, they aren't 'trying to'... they're being themselves and bringing their best. They're acknowledged for who they are.

Delivers – More than you can imagine. When you're building, you're in the hard work phase. It doesn't look pretty. Sometimes we can lose sight of the vision we started with, but your consistent action and insight will move you forward more than you're seeing at the time.

Success - I looked across an Asian city recently and asked myself, what's the learning here, in this scene? Then the 'awkward moment of nothingness' – unemotional, disconnected – simply observing... as I looked at the contrast between the small, old one and two storey homes and the new skyscrapers surrounding them, I began to think about capacity. I imagined the conversations of people who've seen change occurring around them – and the various decisions they could be making.

When we stay comfortable with what's always worked, we limit our capacity. We build to increase capacity – more lives are changed, more customers served, more people and environments served. Building is challenging, but we have an opportunity to dig deep and create solid foundations that will serve many. The increased capacity makes an ever-increasing difference.

That's my understanding of success. To have served well, to know that you've made a positive difference and continue to do so.

Building takes time. There are some things you can do quickly, but don't let people or circumstances rush you in those times when you know you need to take the time to listen, to ask, to learn. I grew up on a farm. I've seen firsthand that seeds also take a long time to grow to their potential. And their potential isn't just the crop that's sold for food, it's the seeds planted for the next harvest. They're tiny, take a long time to grow, but when they're nurtured well the increase is incredible. It usually takes longer than we want it to, but our patience pays off.

If you know you're growing your dream and increasing your capacity, you don't need to be distracted or discouraged by the expectations of others. They don't see your foundations. They don't know the seeds you've planted. Seeds have been planted that come to fruition – sometimes when you least expect it, and in bigger, more beautiful ways than you can imagine.

Business building – it's all about service. Your business serves your community, customers and staff – and your dreams.

Better life

Life is a journey... keep moving forward.

Do and reflect. Learn from your doing. Do what other people shy away from. Do talk to strangers, do what other people don't bother to do. Do speak up (respectfully) when others don't. Reflect on what you can learn from these moments. When you keep 'having a go' you continue to learn and improve. Stay curious.

Learn from people of all ages. Learn as you go. So many people want to get it right first, get all the information and then take action. This is important in some areas, but many times, the learning and equipping happen along the way. So get on your way.

Travel. There's nothing like new places and new people to keep your thinking fresh and your heart open to others. When you're not travelling, be open to travellers and people who've migrated to your area.

Doing, learning, travelling and reflecting on all of your experiences can help you to understand yourself and others more. Understanding yourself and your strengths positions you to live boldly and authentically, which is the most challenging undertaking in life.

E. E. Cummings expressed it like this...

> 'To be nobody but yourself, in a world that is doing its best, night and day, to make you everybody else – means to fight the hardest battle which any human being can fight, and never stop fighting.'

Others will have their expectations of who you are and how you should show up in the world. But I've found that expectations are exhausting – far more than this battle of discovering and being your true self. Keep learning, doing, and being true to who you are.

Better world

Be a difference maker.

Be focused on helping others as you go throughout your life. Don't leave it until you're older, more settled, more comfortable. Be a giver always. Speak up for those who cannot speak for themselves. As A. A. Milne wrote in 'Winnie The Pooh':

> 'Promise me you'll always remember: You're braver than you believe, and stronger than you seem, and smarter than you think.'

Use your bravery, strength and smarts for the greater good.

Leave the place better than you found it. This is ageless wisdom that can be applied anywhere, and one that tidy people love from a practical perspective. But we can apply this to people also. Consider how you can leave people in a better way than they were when you found them. You may not see in yourself the capacity to make a massive difference, but any positive difference can mean the world to someone.

A smile and a friendly greeting can be all the encouragement someone needs to keep going, it can be an assurance that there is still good in the world, when they're having a moment of feeling that there isn't.

The line between success and failure can be very thin, and encouragement makes a world of difference. Indeed, it is often the one thing that finally gets someone over the line.

Cheering you on,
Kerrie.

Understand yourself and embrace difference

Based in Australia, Kerry Howard AKA Ms Pink Herself is:

- A psychologist, executive coach, entrepreneur, mother, daughter and luminary. She has worked with 500+ clients to improve their sense of self and find their joy in life
- Releasing her first book at the end of 2016 – the culmination of her life's work in the Personal Transformation space
- Absolutely passionate about helping people to experience their best life, even when they are not sure it is possible
- A charismatic keynote presenter. She draws on her own life experiences and practice to deliver powerful messages in a truly authentic way - presenting on a diverse range of topics including women in business, personal growth, relationships, health and wellbeing, trauma, career transition and life transformation

Here is the advice she would give to her grandchildren...

Better business

Follow your passion!

Make a business out of the thing you love most, or are most interested in, as it is really very difficult to commit yourself to the demands of running a business if you do not enjoy what you are doing every day.

Finding your passion can be quite a difficult thing to do, though, especially when you are young. It is also important to understand that over our lifetime our interests, and therefore our passions, will change... so don't be afraid to move on from your business when the passion for it starts to wane and you find yourself with a new interest.

You are a creative and inspiring individual and your business, when based on your passion, will always reflect that creativity. As a result, your passion and creativity will allow you to inspire those around you.

Better life

Love does NOT conquer all!

We are raised to believe that we have a soul mate in the world somewhere and we are destined to find him or her and live happily ever after...

Perhaps there is, and perhaps you will.

But if you really want to know how to achieve long-term success in an intimate relationship, you have to recognise that love does not conquer all things - we really need to check if we share values, beliefs, behaviours and attitudes to ensure the success of our relationships.

Even when you are young, if you believe that one day you might like to marry or make a long term commitment to the person that you are dating, it is essential that you spend some time exploring some of the 'key' areas of married life before you contemplate formalising that commitment.

You need to understand your partner's values, about money, assets, leisure time, children and their education, working life and career progression, travel and ideals of home life. Along with where you want to live, how you expect to live there and the obligations that all of these decisions place on you as the individuals within your relationship.

You need to know your love languages and know how to show the other one that you love them in 'their' love languages, and they commit to reciprocating.

A long-term intimate relationship is like a business partnership with sex thrown in. You would never go into a business relationship with someone without understanding their vision and plans for the future of the business, their aspirations, their time commitment to the business and their financial contribution and how this compares with your own vision. You compare this with your own contribution and determine the percentage of ownership of the business accordingly.

An intimate relationship also requires this level of analysis to ensure it is successful. This is not 'un-romantic' or overly analytical. It is simply an insightful way to ensure the long-term success of your union, and provides a loving and stable environment for the next generation.

Love enhances all of our values, attitudes, beliefs and behaviours... which is why we need to ensure a shared understanding of what ours are, and if they are compatible with the person you love.

Better world

Eliminate unnecessary judgement in every area of your life, and encourage those around you to do the same... this will make the world a better place!

More specifically, seek to eliminate the unnecessary judgement without compassion that people make about others. If we could rid the world of people judging others unnecessarily, then I believe there would be a greater sense of acceptance between human beings.

Think of how wonderful it would be if different groups within the world stopped using judgement to justify how they treat each other.

The determination that one group is better than or different to another, and therefore needs to be oppressed, is a sentiment that I would love you to try your hardest to eradicate.

We need to remove the attitude that says 'My way is better than your way, and if you don't do it my way, then I'm going to attack you'.

Wouldn't it be wonderful if we lived in a world where nobody had to experience one group deciding what another group should believe in, or not believe in, and if they don't agree then they're going to attack them to make them conform.

Wouldn't it be amazing if we could live in a world where there was open and honest acceptance of everybody's choice to live their life the way that they want to live it, as long as what they're doing doesn't negatively impact on those around them. If there were true acceptance of the fact that individuals, and the groups to which they belong, can choose how they wish to live.

Acceptance that allows individuals to choose how they present themselves in society and to the world, without other people looking at them, judging them, finding shortcomings and then trying to make them change.

I would love it if we could live in a world where we simply accept people for who they are, how they want to live and we do not try to change them. Instead we are open, accepting and embracing of their difference.

A world in which we follow the ODE – Open, Different, Embrace.

Fail, challenge and smile

Based in Singapore, Kristy is:

- Founder and CEO of global brand experience agency, Rebel & Soul
- Managing Director and franchise owner of Quintessentially Events & Weddings Singapore
- Author of 'Positive interactions: How to create memorable event experiences'
- Campaign Asia Woman to Watch 2016
- British Chamber of Commerce finalist in SME Excellence 2016
- A Buy1Give1 Business for Good Champion

Here is the advice she would give to her grandchildren...

Better business

I grew up in a world that had a tendency to point out people's flaws more than their strengths. My school report card regularly read 'could do better', 'dreamer' and 'lacks application'. I'm not sure how many people in this world could honestly 'apply' themselves to a 2-hour advanced mathematics lesson because after an hour of theory, where letters and numbers collide only to form more letters and numbers, my brain pleaded with me to spontaneously combust. I hear report cards are geared a little more toward the positive these days but in general people's encouragement of others is not as prevalent as needed.

Often not content with themselves or their lives, people can be cruel to others. Friends can put you down, parents can discourage without necessarily meaning to, and those who don't know you can be quick to pass scathing judgment.

I was a sensitive soul growing up and one negative word sat with me for days, and the thoughts it conjured for years.

So when it came to leaving university and entering the world of work, I had a sack of negative goodies I could pull out at any time to gift to myself. As a young and naïve little being I had absolutely no sense whatsoever of what I was passionate about (well nothing work-related anyway). Where should I go and what should I do? I had absolutely not a clue.

I went to a wonderful school, but our careers department was a little lacking. At age seventeen I took the mandatory work suitability test. The test deemed that both I, and half the class, were best suited to a life as farmers, librarians and prison wardens. I'm still not entirely sure of the correlation between any of those professions. Perhaps if you're reading this and you know someone in all three you could enlighten me?

Then came the university system, which didn't appear to encourage my passion for anything other than enjoying social engagements helped along by alcohol. The socialising still remains a passion but it didn't give me the confidence or the steer in a career path I was looking for. I studied fairly hard (in between pub sessions) and proudly walked out with a 2:1. However, despite my achievements, it was the soul-destroying words of my Business Studies tutor Mrs Moffat that stayed with me. When she passed me a marked up paper in my third year I could see that my score was good and I was over the moon. My elation was short-lived. It was her final comment that stayed with me for years... 'I really enjoyed your paper Kristy, although I do understand that it must have been terribly difficult for you, English being your second language'.

My jaw hit the floor. A large lump appeared in my throat and any hope of being a success in any discipline disappeared in my mind faster than Usain Bolt off a starting line. She might well have said brilliant examples Castleton, just a shame you wrote the response in hieroglyphics. I was so embarrassed that I couldn't bring myself to tell her I was British born and bred. In fact, I was so mortified that until recently I haven't shared that story with anyone.

Mrs Moffat wasn't the only person in my life that pulled me down. I could tell you a hundred similar stories of people that 'advised' me that I wouldn't make a success of business and I was best working for someone else. Suggestions came in thick and fast that writing was best left to the literary, that moving overseas was career suicide, that life was tough and best tackled cautiously and that any other way would lead to failure. To each of my 'advisers' I say thank you. Thank you for telling me no, can't, won't, shouldn't, wouldn't and couldn't.

To each of them I say thank you.

Thank you for annoying me just enough that I decided to fight a little harder. Thank you for starting a little ambitious fire in my belly. Thank you for constantly challenging my 'why' so that I knew that I was on the right track and thank you, because in trying to prove you wrong, I gained tenacity, wisdom and courage. Thanks to Mrs Moffat, I read more literature. I found writers I liked and looked into their style and why it worked. I asked more questions and I put into practice what I had learnt.

To my grandchildren, I hope, at times, you are discouraged too. I hope you are told no. I hope many people tell you you're crazy, that your ideas will never work, that there is safety in numbers and that you will fail. I hope sometimes you lose. I hope sometimes you fail. I hope you embarrass yourselves.

Some of the most successful people in life have experienced losing many times and had some spectacular fails. In losing and in failing we learn. We learn how to lose and fail gracefully, how to cope with losing and failing and how to imagine winning harder. I hope it will also teach you to appreciate the winning so much more.

So embrace failure.

Give discouragement a big hug.

Laugh in the face of embarrassing moments.

Own every negative in your life because used correctly these negatives can be an incredible driving force in whichever business you chose. And if you meet any Mrs Moffat's along the way give them a hug from me.

Better life

I am fondly looking forward to the day when I have grandchildren running rings around me repeatedly questioning anything and everything that they come into contact with. I have no doubt that my own grandparents found it cute the first few times - and beyond frustrating the next fifty times - when I bullied them for answers to my never ending repertoire of inquisitions.

These generally ranged from 'why do I have to share the chocolate cake?' (The whole cake, not the slice... I had a very 'healthy' appetite for one so small), to 'why can't I drive your car?' (I was eight and my go kart driving was impeccable; the natural step up was the Volvo sports injection turbo) to 'why can't I make it stop raining?' (My grandmother was Welsh where they have more than their fair share of rainfall, which often had a terribly negative impact on my playtime).

They were all innocent questions, but none of them lacking in insight.

There was nothing physically stopping me from eating the whole cake. In fact, in doing so (and no doubt feeling rather sick afterwards), I would have probably curbed my current passion for the sweeter things in life.

I could also physically operate a go kart. It would only have taken an adapted vehicle and a few lessons to master the full size sports car. There was just a 'minor' law then standing in the way of me and the open roads.

The third question is perhaps the most intriguing. People in the world would have told me, and would tell me today, that stopping the rain is impossible. I can still hear my grandmother's interpretation of Mother Nature and how she controls the weather fronts by turning the sun, the moon and the tides on and off every day. Yet, having travelled extensively, I have since met thousands of people that have now told me that we can control the rain.

On one end of the spectrum there are the Indonesian Pawang Hujans who are religiously called in to bless every harvest or family celebration to ensure the rains don't fall for the event. I have had the wonderful pleasure of being present at a number of these events, some in the middle of Indonesia's wet season. I have personally experienced the intense rain clearing just moments before the events start. Call it what you will and believe it or not, I know who I will have on speed dial for all my future parties.

At the other end is a more scientific and calculated response to rain control, seeding. Used in hot countries to counteract drought, and in countries with high rainfall to encourage dry spells for events, the seeding of clouds is a chemical-induced process that forces rain when you want it rather than when you don't. It's ethics and ecological benefits may well be in question, but it proves that my question had insight. And, more importantly, it proved that what was once thought impossible is actually possible after all.

There are a wealth of examples that prove the same point.

We thought we had to walk from A to B and then we invented the wheel. We went on to invent the train, which helped to eradicate starvation in many countries by transporting food to where it was most needed. We believed the plague would infect and destroy the world, and then we learnt how it was carried and how to inhibit its spread. We thought that we needed to be in a room to connect with someone, and then we invented the telephone. It didn't stop there. Then we took connectivity so much further and invented the Internet. We thought it was impossible to fly and then we flew astronauts to the moon.

Challenging the status quo creates a future of possibilities.

So my piece of advice to my grandchildren is to question and to challenge.

Challenge everything you see and feel. Challenge what anyone does, says or believes. Because without that our future progress will be stifled.

Challenge your grandchildren in the same way too, so that we can all look forward to a day when every generation of our family exists in one time, to continue to run rings around each other and challenge the future together.

Better world

Over the years, life has thrown me many good experiences and several challenging ones. There were the vanity pains in puberty, where my skin erupted and my teeth resisted any movement from metal plates stuck hard and fast to them for over two years. The boy pains in my teens, where initially I wasn't attracting them due to, in part, the mouth full of metal. Subsequently I did attract them... only for them to be enticed away by another girl a week later. The early twenties pain was breaking my leg in multiple places and spending nine months on crutches. The thirties pain was years of dealing with Myalgic Encephalomyelitis (no, I can't pronounce it either – lets just call it my sleepy patch).

None of these challenges were life threatening. But as a youngster, unskilled in life's adversities, they were incredibly hard on me at the time, and required a fair amount of work on my part to overcome them.

It continues to surprise me that schools don't teach more about overcoming life's challenges.

We still have such an academically driven education system. Academia makes up for such a small part of what life throws at us, yet the system rarely provides us with the tools with which to cope. It's lovely knowing the detail about cumulus cloud formations, cumulus derived from the Latin for heap, but it doesn't really help me on a personal cloudy day. It's an achievement knowing the difference between a transitive and intransitive verb, but it's not something I like to point out when someone is throwing insults at me using the wrong conjugation.

I'm sure the schooling system has changed since I was there. I hope that coping skills are now learnt from a young age, letting kids understand

and embrace their individuality instead of shying from difficult situations or overreacting. That wasn't quite the case when I was growing up.

The only non-textbook knowledge we were shown on the human body was from a 1960's video on menstruation and the only practical application was how to apply a condom to a range of crudité vegetables in one biology class. Dinner party nibbles have never been quite the same since.

Having travelled extensively, and looking back, my first day at school felt like a visit to a foreign country. The place, the smells and the attire, were all new and all a little bit strange. Even though the teachers and pupils appeared to be speaking English, I didn't really understand any of their terminology. I was scared, unsure as to how I would fit into this place and I lost my tongue. Luckily, when that happened, I was six years old and the beautiful thing at that age is that you don't need words. Children are wonderfully accepting and forgiving, and you only need to give them one thing to keep encouraging them:

A smile.

When I didn't respond to the other kids, they smiled and they kept on smiling until I felt compelled to smile back. Then I wanted to smile too.

Charles Darwin was one of the first people to document smiling as a science. He recognised that other nonverbal forms of conversation such as body language or gestures differ from country to country, whilst the smile remains universal.

Smiling is a language that everyone understands regardless of their past, their present or their future. Regardless of their age, their nationality, their situation or their state. It breeds positivity, confidence and love. It can be given and it can be received, anywhere and anytime, by and to anyone. It doesn't cost one cent. But it pays. And it keeps on paying for as long as it's remembered.

Smiling saved me from crumbling in the playground from six to sixteen. It saved me from the pain of the break ups, the broken legs and the years stuck in my sleepy patch. Smiles fixed a thousand of my woes and will fix a thousand more.

If those saving smiles weren't enough to convince me to smile more, then medical research certainly is. It's widely known that smiling reduces stress through the release of endorphins. It also reduces your heart rate and temporarily reduces your blood pressure. One study even found that regular smiling increases our lives by an average of seven years. That's one paper I'll be marking for the attention of my life insurance premiums manager.

In the film Annie, the lyrics to one of my favourite songs read 'you're never fully dressed without a smile'. There are many ways to smile, but it's important to put on the right one to get the positive health-inducing benefits. French neurologist Guillaume Duchenne identified two types of smile: the Duchenne smile, where both corners of the mouth raise up and the cheek movement forms crows feet, and the non-Duchenne where only one of the muscle groups moves to form more of a grimace, fearful or nervous smile. The Duchenne induces trust and empathy, is highly contagious and makes you more attractive. Miss a muscle group however and you may appear embarrassed, fake or wildly enigmatic like the Mona Lisa.

So to my beautiful grandchildren, smile and smile warmly and openly.

Find something to smile about daily. First smile for yourself and then share that smile. Seek out those who need smiles. Share it with those who need it the most or for those who are not easy to smile for. Find out what would make them smile and work hard to make those smiles happen. For those smiles are worth a thousand of those who don't need it so much.

Smile to encourage.

And smile to help bring peace.

For smiling is infectious. And I would love nothing more than for you to help spread a global smiling epidemic.

Be systematic about learning from mistakes

Based in Australia, Kylie is:

- A Chartered Accountant and Director, RJS Accounting Services
- A Co-Founder and Director of Free To Shine Ltd, a registered charity that believes children should be in schools not in brothels
- Winner of the 2013 PAN Community Contributions by an Accounting Business Award
- Winner of the 2016 B1G1 Grand Giving Award
- A firm believer that people with passion can change the world for the better

Here is the advice she would give to her grandchildren...

Better business

The most important thing to understand in business is that mistakes aren't all bad.

Sure, some are more dramatic than others. But you must learn from each and every one. And you will make plenty of them over the years, there is nothing surer in life.

The lessons that you learn from these mistakes will make you a better business person, a better leader and a better teacher to those around you.

Explore in detail what went wrong. Why and how did it happen? And - after fixing it this time - what strategies or systems must you implement to ensure that it doesn't happen again?

Be sure that your whole team are aware of the issue – both the reason (not an excuse) that the mistake happened and what you now know to be the correct and best way to address the problem going forward. This may feel a little like a confession – hopefully not a public execution – but it is vitally important for the business to have it aired and dealt with throughout the team.

The bigger the mistake... the bigger the lesson. And I know from experience that you'll never make the same mistake again!

Better life

Written first in the 1700's, the adage that there is nothing certain in life besides death and taxes remains true to this day – and to your current day too, I'm sure. Taxes can be minimised (PS - find yourself a great accountant). But the other aspect of the quotation is harder to comprehend.

At any stage in life dealing with the death of people you love is incredibly difficult.

Having lost my husband at a relatively young age (36), what I learned is that you must tell the people you love that you love them. Yes, my grandsons (and granddaughters), that means OUT LOUD, and at every opportunity.

You never know when they may not be around. Which is why I have decided that, if the last thing that someone hears from me is 'I love you', then I'll be at peace with that.

Too many people have regrets about their last conversation with those that have passed. PLEASE don't be one of these people. It is a terrible regret to have to live with, and one that is so easy to avoid.

Surround yourself with people you love and that love you in return – remembering it's not quantity but quality that matters in all aspects of your life.

Better world

This is a much harder piece of advice for me to formulate for you, my grandchildren.

I do hope that, by the time you're reading this, some of the issues in our world will have settled down. But I fear that that may be stretching reality - even with my level of optimism.

Edmund Burke once, correctly in my opinion, said 'the only thing necessary for the triumph of evil is for good men to do nothing'.

There are so many things wrong with our world, and you can't tackle them all. So the important thing for you to do is to find the one thing that you are most passionate about, and then work towards making that better.

For me, that passion is to end sex trafficking. I cannot sleep properly each night knowing there are children enslaved and tortured for the sole purpose of someone else's 'pleasure'.

I am sure that you will all be 'good men' and find the issue that lights you up, be it the environment, animal welfare or world peace (aim high!)

Believe me, making a small difference to that one issue will help to change the world. And, importantly, it will also change you and those around you too. What seems to be a small thing to you – perhaps only taking a little of your time and/or money – will have a ripple effect that will surprise you and should make you proud of yourself.

Do something positive, do it well, and your impact will be felt around the world.

Live a life of congruence

Based in Singapore, Louisa is:

- A serial entrepreneur, thought leader and change advocate in reforming Healthcare and Education.
- Co-founder of DP Dental – a 30 person global boutique practice working closely with B1G1 because they believe that every business should be a Business of Giving.
- A member of the advisory board of the Imagine Cambodia Foundation
- A speaker, coach and consultant, with a firm belief in congruent leadership rooted in strong core values
- Founder of Progressive Practice, and author of 'Progressive Practice: Disrupt yourself before others do'

Here is the advice she would give to her grandchildren...

Better business

TRUST is the first thing you need to establish between you and your clients, between you and your business partners and also between you and your team members.

To be a trustworthy business means to keep to your word and deliver to your promise.

I always tell my team members there is no boss in the business - but if you really need to know who pays the bills and is the boss, then that person is none other than our clients.

Typical organisation charts are pyramidal, with the Founder / CEO at the top, then middle management followed by everyone else.

In my 'organisational chart', it starts with a circle with the word 'Client' in the middle, from which stems all the other clusters of the team, grouped according to their function. They surround the clients and work towards giving the solution needed by the client.

Trust between the business and the client is established when what you say is reflected in what you do.

How do you gain trust in a short space of time from your clients, business partners and team members?

Live a life of congruence. Align your own personal values to that of your business.

All aspects of your business must also be congruent. If you say you are a progressive business, then you must make sure that you are progressive in all aspects of the business. You will need to have adopted the latest technology in your field to deliver the latest ideologies. Likewise you must have kept abreast with the latest in marketing trends and be managing with the latest in management philosophies.

What are the key values that you need to adhere to in business? Well, to me, honesty and integrity are the most important.

Seek to always deliver excellence in whatever you do, and to constantly seek to improve and better yourself. Always give your very best and the monetary rewards will follow naturally, because your clients can sense your commitment to providing them with the very best.

LISTEN to your clients and their needs and always be flexible and open to changes.

Never give up learning and improving on your knowledge. Education is the best investment that you can ever make.

Remember, the journey of entrepreneurship is like being on a travelator that is going backwards... you have to keep moving and evolving or you will be left behind!

Better life

Live a life of CONGRUENCE in order to live a life optimally.

Every one of us is born with a gift. It is our life's aim to discover this gift, which we may then use to contribute to a greater cause and create a positive impact to others with our time on Earth.

In order that this quest for our greater purpose not be hindered, we need to lead life in its simplest form, that which takes the least amount of effort. This is possible if, for starters, we lead a life that is CONGRUENT.

What does it mean to be congruent in life?

It is that one's ideal and actual self must match. What you aspire to be is what you already are and often the only hindrance to that is our own belief of what we are and can be.

Next, one's internal self and the external self must also match. It is very tiring to be wearing many faces for the different situations.

Practice congruence and you will realise how your life is a lot more simplified and less tiring to maintain.

What are the key values that you need to adhere to in life?

In life, we are surrounded by people whom we seek to build meaningful relationships with. To people around you, always seek to be KIND and COMPASSIONATE.

Many people look but do not SEE. Always seek to extend kindness and compassion – in what you say and in what you do, to the strangers on the street but most importantly to the people whom we often take the most for granted, those closest to us – our family.

Be mindful, present and relate to others always with full focus and attention. That is how we stay connected and deepen our relationships.

Better world

Live always thinking of others – the people around you now and the people who will be in the world long after you are gone. That will ensure that you live responsibly.

Once you have attained the ability to live the simplified life of CONGRUENCE, you will find that you have the time to then live a life thinking about how you can contribute to the well-being of others.

When you do something that makes you yourself happy, that happiness is only enjoyed by one person in the world. When you do something that makes one other person happy, two people enjoy that happiness. When you start a movement that positively impacts many other people, imagine the happiness level that you have just elevated.

What are the key values that you need to adhere to that would make the world a better place to live in?

Firstly, SUSPEND ALL JUDGEMENT. We often bring our previous experiences into our interaction with another person. We make assumptions and are bogged down by prejudices. Always approach each conversation with another person on a clean slate. Forget all previous opinions you may have formed of the person and just be focused on the present. The same applies when we talk to strangers, but start to apply our previous encounters of people of the same nationality, religion, or race and impose prejudices onto this new person. Remember, everyone is an individual in their own right. Suspend all judgement and you will be surprised to find the many commonalities we all have as one human species.

Secondly, practice EMPATHY. Always put yourself in the shoes of the other person. Give people the benefit of the doubt and when in doubt, err on the positive side.

So, my dear grandchild, I write to you here a snippet of what I have spent the last 40 years of my life discovering and I know that as long as I continue to keep my mind open and my heart grateful to all the blessings that I am receiving every day, I will be able to continue to work towards passing on my legacy in this world, the world that you shall inherit.

I will do my best right now to make sure that it will be a world worth inheriting.

The three-part formula for making everything better

Based in Singapore, Masami is:

- Founder of the global giving initiative Buy1Give1 (B1G1)
- Creator of the Impact Test
- Author of the book 'GIVING BUSINESS - Creating Maximum Impact in a Meaning-driven World'

Here is the advice she would give to her grandchildren...

Better business

The primary aim of a business is to become the extension of meaningful human connections.

Businesses should exist to make our life and our world better and greater. Your business can do so by adding great value and meaning to you, to the people you serve and to the world.

It's easy to forget that businesses are here to create greater **meaning**, not just more value for their customers or more money for their stake-holders. In earlier times, many businesses focused purely on the maximisation of transactions and profits because doing that was the way for businesses to survive. Business leaders were selected and promoted based on short-term financial performances. As a result, our businesses created many issues and consequences like environmental destruction, lack of trust in the marketplace and unfair living conditions for many. This was a big mistake.

Running a business or working for a business became simply a means to earn a living and to create greater financial prosperity. And with this approach, many lost their aspirations.

But we have come to learn that there is a better way. We have learned that businesses have enormous potential to create great change in our world, far more than anything else can. And we can really enjoy the time we spend in and on our businesses as our life's work.

So, to make sure we do not repeat the same mistakes we made in the past, please always remember to do these three things:

1. Create and build businesses you love

2. Create and build businesses others love

3. Create and build businesses that are good for the world

When you do all of these things, you will always be fulfilled in your business journey.

And our world will continue to be a great place for all of us to belong to.

Better life

Remember that a joyful life is created through this simple formula:

$$Acceptance\ (Past) + Trust\ (Future) = Love\ (Present)$$

Acceptance

Accept what has happened. What happened in the past cannot be changed no matter how hard you try. But the action you take now is totally under your control. Also accept others for who they are. You cannot change others by judgment and confrontation. But you can inspire others to become greater by you living the greatest life you can live.

Acceptance gives you a peaceful mind. And a peaceful mind gives you great focus to make the best decisions you can make, every moment, every day.

Trust

Trust others. When you trust, you create a trusting environment for everyone to thrive.

We all have weaknesses but trust makes us stronger. Even when there is a lack of trust in the environment, be the one to be trusted. Be open, vulnerable and authentic regardless of the situation. And trust your future. You cannot predict your future 100 per cent. Hence, your life should not be limited by your assumptions. Any mistakes and hardships you experienced in the past do not dictate your future. And what others tell you does not limit your future potential. Also remember that you never know how many more days you have left to be here. So, do the best you can today.

Love

Finally, love the present moment. The present moment is the only thing that is ever real (and it's a gift; a real 'present' in every sense). Right now, you can only directly change the present moment, not your past and future. You are fully in control of how you feel, what you think and what you do right now at this present moment. It is the most powerful moment of your life.

When you accept the past and trust the future, you are more likely to love your present moment. Equally, when you live your life fully and love the present moment, you can naturally accept others and the things around you and have positive anticipation for the future too.

Better world

Sometimes, we feel small and powerless in the great scheme of things. It feels like what we do at an individual level does not make much of a difference.

But remember that the **small differences you make today are more powerful than the big things you hope to achieve one day**.

Care. Connect. Innovate for greatness. Be grateful for what you have today. Love others for who they are. Dream. Persevere with belief. Become better than yesterday. Share what you have with others generously. Solve a problem right in front of you. Smile more. Be humble. Take care of small things. Be open-minded and innocent. And enjoy.

Today and every day, commit to make the world a better place for all.

Have an adventure

Based in Australia, Nicky:

- Has a background in psychology, teaching and coaching
- Is the Managing Director of Free To Shine, a registered charity that believes children should be in schools not in brothels
- In 2009 she spent a month with survivors of sex trafficking in Cambodia
- She was then given a weekly radio show to raise awareness of the issue, and
- Went on to establish Free To Shine, which to date has enrolled 700 high risk girls in education to prevent them being targeted by sex traffickers

Here is the advice she would give to her grandchildren...

Better business

Do something that really matters - You want to finish a day of working knowing that you spent the day well, that you utilised your talents and skills, that you were challenged, knowing that you gave the best of you and that you cannot imagine doing anything else. You want to know that you spent your day doing something that really matters.

Doing something that really matters will of course challenge you. Be very clear on why you are doing what you are doing and how it makes the world a better place - and this will carry you through every challenge and obstacle you encounter. You will literally find a way to walk over the hot coals.

I found myself promising survivors of sex trafficking that I would find girls in rural villages who aren't in school and help them go to school so that they aren't trafficked. I had never been to a rural village and had no idea how to fulfil such a promise!

And then I found myself at a seminar that I did not know included a fire-walk! A quick Google search told me that my skin is like paper and should burn, and that my blood is predominantly water and should boil. I pictured children trapped in a brothel cell, looking at me, their arms outstretched through the bars, as I literally found a way to walk over hot coals to get to them.

I knew in that moment that no matter the obstacle, challenge or difficulty, I would do whatever it took.

As the Managing Director of an organisation that has so far kept 700 girls safe from being trafficked, the challenges and obstacles are sometimes enormous and they come thick and fast. Often we haven't finished dealing with one issue or problem when the next one is already upon us. But knowing we are doing something that really matters keeps us focused, and keeps us determined to do whatever it takes.

Do something that really matters and you will always find a way.

Better life

Have an adventure - We live in an incredible world, with so much beauty and so much to be explored. Hike some mountains, swim some streams, see the world, fly a plane, watch the dolphins. Whatever excites and challenges you, do it. Really, truly make the most of your life.

We are so lucky to have the opportunities we have. When I was five I went on a plane for the first time. I was invited into the cockpit to meet the pilot. He showed me a couple of buttons to press and a lever to push. Wow - I was helping to fly the plane!

That flight was my first trip overseas. We were going to Spain. It was incredible. I rode a donkey up a mountain, and at a restaurant we passed each day the waiter would rush over to give me a free ice cream, and I learnt to say 'la cuenta por favor'. It was another world. I learnt at five that there was a big wide world out there, where some things are done the same and other things are done differently. I wanted to explore the world.

When I left England, I spent a year living in a little Greek village on the outskirts of a little Greek town. One evening I ordered a beer without realising every one of my Greek friends had ordered a coffee – they put it down to me being British! When their friends arrived I was introduced as a 'real life vegetarian!' Living in another culture is one of the greatest adventures and greatest privileges.

Mum and I decided to spend 6 weeks on a motorbike island hopping. It was the best! I packed 3 sets of swimmers, 3 t-shirts and shorts, and 6 books into a little side box, along with our tent and off we set to the ferry to take us to the first island. I discovered the old town of Rhodes; I hiked the deepest gorge in Europe; we pulled to the side of the road to let all the goats pass; we visited old towns and ruins, and swam in little lakes and streams. It was incredible.

On my way to Australia, I spent a few months exploring a little more of the world; I hiked mountains in Canada, swamps and volcanoes in Hawaii, glaciers in New Zealand, I drove a monster truck school bus over crushed cars and did aerobatics in a red bull plane over a lake.

It is the adventures I've had that shaped me, taught me and made me grow. I wouldn't be doing what I'm doing today if I hadn't had the adventures I've had.

Have an adventure!

Better world

Do something, but do it properly - I considered some of the problems of the world; sexual abuse of children, environmental destruction, child marriage, poverty, animal abuse, human trafficking... There are so many issues and it's hard to know where to start.

The good news is you don't have to solve all the world's problems - there are 7 billion of us, so if we all just pick one then we'd solve them all, so it doesn't matter which one you choose, just choose.

I asked myself, 'of all the problems that exist, which do I think is the worst, which problem can I simply not come to terms with living in a world with?' For me the answer was clear, I cannot live in a world where children are enslaved in the commercial sex industry, raped and tortured repeatedly every day.

In my first month with survivors of sex trafficking I was taken to the home of a group of sex workers. We were there to give them soap and condoms - and by doing so each month, learn when underage girls came from the countryside to engage in sex work. The women rolled out a mat across what floor boards there were and I tried to position myself on a piece of floorboard so that I wouldn't fall through one of the many holes into the dirty stagnant lake water that sat a few feet below. We sat in a circle, while the pimps stood at the door, deciding how long we could talk and what we could talk about. One woman breastfed her baby while we talked, a small child played beside his mum, and two teenage girls, aged 13 and 14, had indeed recently joined the group from the countryside.

The team I was accompanying had told me, 'be ready to run, if we have to.' I had a million thoughts racing through my head. When the team had finished their conversation, they turned to me, the visitor, and asked if I had any questions. I did, of course I did. But something stopped me and I became acutely aware that I had been welcomed into these women's homes, complete with children playing and pimps at the door. Instead, I said, 'first, do they have any questions they'd like to ask me?' They did.

- 'What country was I from?'

- 'Was it very different to Cambodia?'

- 'Did women do sex work in Australia?'

- 'Did men sometimes trick them, and pretend there was only one man but when they got inside the room there were actually 3 men waiting and they beat her up and raped her, did this ever happen in Australia, because it had just happened to her and she was angry and upset?'

I learnt more from their questions than asking my own. And what I've learned since is Cambodia is a polite culture, and as the foreigner you'll always be asked if you have any questions. But in that moment they are actually offering you the power. As someone who could afford air travel you are deemed rich, and as such more knowledgeable and more deserving of their respect than they of yours! Please, don't accept the power. Hand the power to them, and ask instead if they have any questions they'd like to ask you. After you've answered their questions, by all means, ask away.

It's not easy knowing how best to help. Many people rush in, armed with good intentions and a desire to help. Don't go in with pre-conceived ideas of what is needed and what you should do. Take time to listen and learn.

Do what works, not what makes you feel good.

This isn't about you, so leave your ego at home. Good intentions aren't good enough. Playing with children in an orphanage isn't actually helpful. Do your research, question, reflect, learn.

Building houses and playgrounds are activities offered to foreigners because they like these activities, even though these foreign volunteers are taking the work of local construction workers who would have been able to afford to send their children to school that day if they'd been given the job instead, not to mention that our eager foreign volunteers lack the local expertise of how to build houses from bamboo and woven palm leaves for example.

Many people focus on the good that they're doing and don't examine the negative footprint they might be leaving behind. Others believe that as long as they're doing more good than harm, then that's ok. I'd argue it's not. It's not OK to make an impoverished community a bit better in one way if you actually unwittingly make it worse in another.

We once took a group of 4 visitors to meet some of the families we work with. One lady, we'll call her Caroline, was especially moved by the people she met. When I wasn't looking, she slipped a grandma a $100 note, thinking she was doing a good thing. She unwittingly undid a year's worth of progress, and put this grandma in danger. We work tirelessly with our families to help them solve the multitude of problems they encounter. We empower them. We never give them money. For 6 months this grandma and her many neighbours, instead of working to solve their problems, asked us for money every time we saw them. Not to mention she just gave someone $100 in a community that rarely has more than a few cents. This woman could have been beaten up for that money!

These are people's lives. They deserve for us to be competent. Commit to getting it right. Hold yourself to high standards.

Do something, but do it properly.

It's all for them

Based in Singapore, Paul Dunn is:

- Chairman and co-founder of the (Buy1Give) B1G1: Business For Good movement
- Author of two books, 'Write Right' (now re-released as 'Write Language') and the best-selling 'The Firm of the Future'
- A global keynote speaker, often referred to as 'The Wizard of Wow', Paul focuses on Creating a Legacy and what he calls 'The stunning power of small'

Here is the advice he would give to his grandchildren…

Better business

In this past year, I've begun a lot of my presentations around the world with a beautiful slide of a butterfly.

Most people see it as a Monarch butterfly.

I put a title alongside it. I tell them it's a FORTHEM Butterfly.

Then I ask if anyone ever gets asked to do presentations AND if they get butterflies when they start? Almost every hand goes up.

'You've got to get those butterflies,' I explain, 'they help your body produce chemicals to strengthen you. But the trick is to get those butterflies flying in formation.'

I ask if it's OK to explain how I get my butterflies flying in formation. I tell the audience how, when I'm being introduced, I always stand at the back on the audience's left of stage side. And I say just 2 words together between 6 and 12 times.

The two words are, 'For them.' So my mantra becomes something like 'For them, for them, for them, for them, for them, for them…'

And so the butterfly on the screen is really a 'FOR THEM' butterfly. It reminds me of how I have to get focused OFF myself and on to them - the audience - how I have to make them the hero of this.

And so it is in business generally. Everything must be for them and never for you.

Every presentation, every sale, every welcome, every piece you ever write... for them, for them, for them.

Better life

And everything you've just read is really about life itself. For them, for them, for them.

For your family: for them, for them, for them.

For your community: for them, for them, for them.

For our world: for them, for them, for them.

Better world

Yes, as you've just read, for our world: for them, for them, for them.

Once we get that, everything changes. Really... everything changes!

Consider, for example, the accountant I was mentoring today. They used to have a Mission Statement that said, in part 'our goal is to help our clients achieve their goals.'

Now it reads like this:

WE HELP OUR CLIENTS VASTLY EXCEED WHAT THEY THOUGHT THEY COULD ACHIEVE SO THAT THEY CAN PLAY A BIGGER GAME WHICH IS THEN REFLECTED IN THEIR FAMILIES, IN OUR COMMUNITY, IN OUR COUNTRY AND IN OUR WORLD.

By firmly believing AND acting on that, we change our world. Well, even more profoundly, you change our world.

And that, dear grandchild, is precisely why you're here.

Have a fabulous journey here... for them, for them, for them.

Do what you love and success will follow

Based in Australia, Peter is:

- A partner at multi-award winning accountants & business advisers, Collins Hume
- Featured in the book 'The world's most inspiring accountants'
- A CPA specialising in business coaching, who has twice been named as one of Australia's Top 40 young business leaders
- An accredited Specialist SMSF Adviser, Business Improvement Adviser and Financial Adviser with a Masters in Business Administration

Here is the advice he would give to his grandchildren...

Better business

I grew up loving the outdoors. As a teenager most afternoons I trained for football, particularly rugby league. But my main passion in my mid-teens was surfing. I loved to go to the beach and, every opportunity I got, I would be there. If my mates and I couldn't get a lift with our parents, we would often ride the 20 kilometres to the coast to get our fix.

When it came to choosing a career I knew I had to find something that would allow me to live and work near the coast. A career that I enjoyed and empowered me to help others, and at the same time allowed me the freedom to pursue the lifestyle I desired. I was never one for crowds and concrete jungles, so I knew at an early age that city life wasn't for me.

I thoroughly enjoyed mathematics, and had a keen interest in business, so I pursued a career that incorporated both. That is why I chose to become an accountant and business adviser. When I finished my secondary schooling not wanting to leave our beautiful area, I gained entry into Southern Cross University and commenced a Bachelor of Accounting and later an MBA.

Whilst studying I worked hard on local farms and at the local dairy co-operative, Norco, to pay my way through university. This hard work made me appreciate the value of money; knowing how hard it is to earn a dollar made me think twice before I spent it on things I didn't really need.

I wasn't frugal - I just didn't want to waste it!

It was a few years later when I starting travelling that this really hit home. Seeing people labouring in the fields doing back breaking labour for a few bucks a day really makes you appreciate how good we have it. I used to complain that fifteen dollars an hour was not even worth working for, but my hourly wage was more than some people made in a week! It was this higher pay rate that enabled me to buy a car at a young age, to travel to different countries and enjoy a great way of life. I'm truly thankful for that.

It was also at an early age that I realised that it wasn't how much money you earned or the material possessions you had, but the life that you lived, that made you a success. If you do what you love, provide for your family and can afford the lifestyle you desire, then I consider you a success.

Many people relate success to wealth or fame. If you Google successful people you will often find images of wealthy business owners or celebrity entertainers.

Perhaps these people are at the top of their chosen field, but are they really content in life?

Equally important is the young girl who always dreamed of having a beautiful family and didn't desire fame or fortune. The young girl had a family, provided for them in any way she could, cared for them and doted over their every need and raised four healthy educated adults. Just as someone who excels in their career, I believe this lady was as successful as anyone else. She achieved her goals and the lifestyle she wished for. This lady was my mother. And just like her, there are so many successful people that live their lives unassumingly, away from the limelight, but are nevertheless great successes in my opinion.

So what can we learn from this in business?

Do what you love and success will follow. Choosing a career that ignites your passion will never become 'work'. Sure, there will be days you'd prefer to stay at home or go to the beach. But doing something you love and are passionate about means you will never begrudge your chosen career.

If you decide on your career purely for money you will never find true happiness or contentment. I'd be naive to say money isn't important. Sure it helps, but true happiness can't be bought. It comes from within.

So my one piece of advice when it comes to business (and perhaps general life) is to do what you love and it will never become mundane or boring. Use your skills, knowledge and passion to positively impact the lives of others and true success will follow.

Fame and fortune doesn't mean you're successful. Having a large bank balance and a flash car doesn't equate to success. Success isn't monetary. It is contentment and happiness in knowing you have done your best with what you have. As Henry Ford once said, 'The whole secret of a successful life is to find out what is one's destiny to do, and then do it.'

Better life

We often hear the common phrases 'life is short', 'you only get one life' or 'you're a long time dead.' There are so many similar sayings and all too often we don't heed this advice or understand the true meaning of these phrases. They are all very true. Life is very short, so let's put it into perspective....

Worldwide the average life expectancy of a person is about 70 years of age. The first 20 are spent as a child or teenager at school and perhaps university. We then join the workforce for the next 40-45 years. We work hard until 60-65, and then retire for 5-10 years. This means that, on average, 60 percent of our lives are spent working and earning a living.

So what is my point?

My point is that it is imperative to spend your life, especially your working life, doing something you love and are passionate about. Something where you feel you are making a difference. Something that doesn't feel like work or a chore.

We all know being a child is fun; we don't have a worry in the world. We all look forward to retirement when we can travel, relax and reflect on our lives. But what about the 40-odd years in between? These years should not be spent going through the motions, wishing your life away for the weekend, your next holiday or even retirement. Once these years are gone, they're gone! You can't get them back. So choose a career that is more than a pay cheque. Make sure you make the most of your time on earth and do the things that bring you joy and happiness.

In my role as an accountant and business adviser I come across many people who are disillusioned with their business. When they started out they had grand visions of making a solid income, working fewer hours, spending more time with their friends and family, taking extended holidays and not having to answer to anyone. Who wouldn't want this, right?

Unfortunately, for most people this isn't the reality. They end up working more hours, juggling their cash flow, being too swamped to enjoy a decent holiday, and are often the lowest paid person in the business with the most stress! Is this how they intended on spending the majority of their life? Is there another way? And how can they resolve this issue?

Any business owner in this situation needs to revisit the reason they started the business. Understand why. What were their original intentions, why did they set out on this path and how can they make their dreams a reality? Are they really passionate about their business and do they feel they can make the world a better place by being in business, or is it a means to an end?

Find out what fuels the fire within! It isn't always easy, but doing what you love and what you are passionate about will make your working life or business less of a chore and more enjoyable.

Since the early days of being an accountant my life motto has always been 'We work to live, not live to work.' I truly believe that by following these simple words of wisdom, and following our dreams to do what we are passionate about, we will ensure our working lives are much more pleasurable and meaningful.

I'm not naïve enough to think there won't be days or moments when you wish you were somewhere else or the stress gets on top of you. No matter what your career, this is part of life, so it's bound to happen. But as a whole, I believe that if you wake up knowing you are going to work, and, as a result, make another's life better in some way, it will be very difficult not to enjoy what you do.

So, remember that 'life is short', do what you love and do it well. You have nothing to lose - ensure you make all your years on earth, from birth to death, meaningful, special and purposeful.

As the old Scottish proverb says, 'Be happy while you're living, for you're a long time dead.'

Life isn't a dress rehearsal so make the most of it, every day.

Better world

An important part of our life's journey lies in contributing to the greater good, being part of something greater than ourselves.

When we consider how one might make the world a better place, images of great leaders of social movements, scientists developing new medicines and vaccines or inventors devising new theories may come to mind. But the reality is that there is plenty of room for less lofty acts to create small measures of happiness in the lives around us. These small gestures strengthen our sense of community, lighten our burdens for a brief moment and give us something to smile about.

All too often I work with people who fixate on their finances. The stress and worry they cause themselves by worrying about meaningless issues is perhaps creating an unhappy life and leading them to an early grave. I often wonder if they had less money and less stress would they be happier? Would giving that money to those in need, and letting go of the never-ending goal of wealth, bring greater happiness? At what point is enough money, enough? Will an extra zero on your bank account bring greater joy to your life and the feeling of contentment?

The wise and inspirational Masami Sato, CEO and Founder of the charitable organisation B1G1, says, 'Giving and getting both create happiness. Getting starts with what we don't have and isn't always in our control. Giving, on the other hand starts with what we already have and is always 100 percent in our control.'

Think about it. When we give we don't just create happiness for the recipient. We create a stronger feeling of enchantment from within ourselves knowing we made a difference to another's life.

It is for this reason I often say, 'There is no use being the richest person in the cemetery.' Others won't remember you for your wealth, they will remember you by the positive impact you have had on their lives, whether for themselves, or others. I am a strong believer that everyone should strive to positively impact as many other people we can in our life and leave a legacy.

Importantly, we don't have to give money to make an impact. Consider the likes of Mother Teresa who offered tender loving care to those in need, the poorest of the poor in India. In each human being she saw a child of God, created for better things; to love and to be loved. And that was what she did. It wasn't money that she offered them, but a feeling of belonging.

Not everyone will achieve the missionary compassion of Mother Teresa, but small gifts of love, care and respect cost nothing and can change a person's life immeasurably.

And it doesn't end there.

Consider the ripple effect that giving a gift or gesture to another could have. Often if we say hello to a stranger and offer a smile it will lift their mood. They in turn will share a smile with another and so on. So your original smile and acknowledgement could indirectly impact on several others without you knowing.

Sir Winston Churchill once said, 'We make a living by what we get, but we make a life by what we give', and we should always remember this throughout our life.

I have always been a strong believer in giving and helping those less fortunate. Knowing the struggle that others have on a day to day basis I have always had a passion to improve their lives in some way, shape or form. I do this on a daily basis with the advice I provide in my occupation. And for those I can't help on a personal level, I often give via charities such as B1G1.

Whilst I always gave personally, I knew there was more I could do. That is why my business partners and I decided to incorporate giving in to our business. Doing this not only increased the difference we could make, but it also gave our team a greater purpose. Knowing that each day they came to work they were directly and positively impacting the lives of others gave them a great sense of achievement and contentment.

The momentum that our giving gained was completely unexpected. Our clients and other local businesses followed our lead, incorporating giving in to their business dealings too. And from a small start, everyone is now engaged and the ripple effect is quite extraordinary. Together we are helping change the world, one person at a time.

I encourage you to travel as much as possible, broaden your horizons, learn from others and experience new cultures. But most importantly I encourage you to give to others, especially those who are less fortunate. What we get from giving will always be greater than what we give. And when we depart this earth people will always remember us for the positive impact we made on their lives.

So give generously in any way you can. No matter how small.

Because together we can help change the world, one-by-one.

The greater the giving, the greater the getting back

Based in Australia, Philip:

- Is a behaviourist who focuses on high performance in individuals, teams and whole organisations
- Works as a coach, facilitator and consultant in performance, change, culture and behavioural marketing
- Has run businesses all around the world, being responsible for over $2 billion in sales
- Has started, incubated and enhanced business in over 100 countries
- Has studied with the world's best on four continents
- Is passionate about helping others play their 'bigger games'

Here is the advice he would give to his grandchildren...

Better business

Simple truths - Business at its most elegant is neither difficult nor complex. Businesses become that way over time, and for the wrong reasons. My advice about business is to keep coming back to core principles that can act as simple truths that bust complexity. From these simple truths, the business that you create can be empowered to do really wonderful things.

Here are four simple truths of business:

1. It is only ever about creating value, rather than 'harvesting wealth'

2. Your worst enemies in business are habit and fear

3. Serve from power, never from powerlessness

4. Lead from anywhere, lead everywhere

Create value - In business, it can be about you, or it can be about your customer and consumer. Organisations that look the wrong way (at themselves) get stuck and fail. Great businesses focus on simply enhancing the customer experience – creating or enhancing the value that their customers or consumers get out of life, in a way that is congruent with what the company does (its purpose).

Businesses that create value bring something to the world.

On the other hand, companies or businesses that are 'looking the wrong way' are attempting to harvest wealth. They want to take wealth that has already been created, and get some of it for themselves. It might be in the form of money, or it might be in the form of fame and prestige. It can even be in the form of 'safety' (keeping the shareholders happy). Regardless of its form, harvesting wealth means finding a way to exploit a situation for your own benefit. This is a shortsighted, and only ever a short run, approach.

Creating value builds the size of the pie. Instead of fighting for smaller and smaller slices of diminishing resources, customers or available cash, change your focus. Decide to create value - to build and leverage, and to expand and transform. We can do this by paying respect to what has come before (honour the legacy), recognising that some resources are finite (operate with broader awareness), and always challenging to find new ways to enhance every aspect of the value the customer or consumer receives (innovate).

As you create value, you share in its rewards. The sharing of value can 'ripple out' beyond your customers and consumers, into the wider community. This provides an ecosystem of benefit, expanding and enhancing, rather than greedy accumulation at the expense of others.

And creating value feels great, attracts great people and loyal customers - and is a sustainable way to be a part of something successful for the long term.

Fight the biggest enemies of your business - The biggest enemies of your business are habit and fear. These two things alone destroy more businesses than anything else.

When you find yourself (or people in your business) saying 'We have always done it that way' as a reason for a strategy or tactic, you know that you are living in the past, and driven by habit. Things evolve, and what worked before may not work again. This is a way to waste your money on things that no longer matter to your customer. It is a way to miss the signals of what is really happening in your market and miss the opportunity to innovate.

On the other hand, when you start hearing people justify actions and decisions with 'But what if we don't?' or 'Well, our competitors are doing it, so we must' – you know that your business is being driven by fear. The basis for your decisions is not on what may be possible or what will occur because of what you can DO, but rather avoiding missing out on what you DON'T. Simply put, you are not in control of your choices. You are relying on avoiding 'missing out'.

If you operate from fear and habit, realise that someone else will not, and you can prepare to be massively disrupted. Fight fear and habit - and use positive, customer-focused insights for making decisions - to avoid this path to failure.

Serve from power - Often people serving customers, clients (or even those they work for in an organisation) think that service is about being a 'slave' to those that they serve. This means that they 'have' to respond to each and every request and demand as if they have no choice. You may even hear people inside the company talking about the customers in unpleasant ways and seeing 'customer service' as a burdensome task.

This frame of mind is more like 'customer-slavery' – where we (and all of our resources) are simply at the beck and call of the customer. This often comes from a scarcity mentality – 'we have no choice but to serve them'; or 'if we don't do everything the customer says, we will lose them'.

True customer service has a different tone - it is about serving from a place of power through *choice* – because you VALUE the experience of the customer (or staff member - or even the boss!), and you have a desire to see that their experience is the best that it can be, because it MATTERS.

It is the *intent* which is critical. Are you operating in a way to offer the minimal support to achieve your outcome, or are you truly focused on serving to the best of your capability and creating real value?

Often, many businesses set out to offer the minimum service that they can, which will ensure that customers will use the service but not complain (too much). They think this saves them money and effort, however it stems from a scarcity mindset. Do everything you can to serve your purpose, your organisation and your customers from a place of power, because you *choose* to, and because doing so *matters* to you. This creates unrivalled value and connectedness for all concerned, and shifts you from a 'wealth harvester' to a 'value creator' – where success is really found.

Lead - You don't have to have a title to be a leader. Whatever scenario you find yourself in, you have the opportunity to lead. When you are clear on your 'bigger purpose' and your values, you can step up and lead. (If you are not sure of your purpose or values, or you don't have standards for how you want to play - then you will never lead even if you have the most powerful title in the organisation).

To be a great leader from anywhere, and you are clear on where you want to lead others, then there are six key actions that will make this possible:

1. **Commitment** - Leaders have to walk the talk. If you are not prepared to behave and act in line with what you expect from others, people will never follow. People watch what you do and place more value on that than what you say.

2. **Communication** - Leaders find ways to communicate what is important. Great leaders over-communicate (normally three times more than you would think) so that their simple key messages are heard and accepted by those they are leading.

3. **Coaching** - If we want to lead people, we have to realise that they will need to change - otherwise they can stay just where they are! Great leaders know how to coach, so that they can help the people across the 'gap' to where they are leading to.

4. **Prioritise** - There are so many things competing for the attention of those we lead. If we want to lead, then we have to be clear about what needs to be prioritised – and prioritise it. In every action, conversation, meeting and effort, what we prioritise will be obvious to those we lead.

5. **Purpose** - When people understand the reason 'why' a change has to occur - why it is important that you lead them somewhere - you create the engagement required to bring them along. Consider how serving the purpose of where you are leading can serve their personal purpose, and you will unlock deep engagement and support for where you are leading.

6. **Passion** - Everyone makes decisions emotionally. Tapping into this unlocks the energy of the people you are leading. Being visibly passionate about the place you are leading people will activate them, and give them a sense of importance around what you are trying to achieve.

We can lead from anywhere. There are so many big and small changes that we can influence by stepping up and choosing to lead. Each small change that we inspire people around and lead to can - one action at a time – change the world.

Better life

The three truths of your life - There are only three truths in life. The first truth of life is that no one makes it out alive. The second truth of life is that they don't build hearses with luggage racks - you go out the way you came in and take nothing with you. The third truth of life is it will be exactly what you make it.

If there were five things I would encourage anyone to consider as they create their experience, they would be:

1. Live beyond tolerance

2. Shine, return to love

3. Responsibility

4. Find what makes you happy

5. Believe in something

Live beyond tolerance - Tolerance is simply not enough. We are taught that we should be 'tolerant' of others, their opinions and beliefs. However, to live a great life, tolerance is just not enough. Tolerance assumes that I can recognize your position and take a condescending, power based view that 'I can tolerate you having that position, being that person or behaving in that way'. Really?

Tolerance implies rigidity in my own view of you and your beliefs; and limits my ability to grow.

Living beyond tolerance means accepting and embracing difference, being OK with being different and wrong, and seeking external challenge to enhance personal growth.

It should never be enough for me to 'tolerate' you, or for you to 'tolerate' me. We are then two rigid, fixed objects that 'look down our noses' at each other from a 'belief' that we are better. We can make up stories for why we should tolerate the other, yet we miss what life is about - creation and learning.

Imagine if - instead of tolerance - you showed humility and openness? Simply being humble enough to realise that the other person may have brilliant reasons for doing or believing, may have experiences that you have never considered and information you have never been exposed to. From this humility - and with an openness to explore their position and the differences between you - you could evolve yourself, your beliefs and your world view to something even more valuable, more nuanced or more complete than it is now.

Tolerance is only a path to limiting yourself, and I encourage you to be so much more.

Shine - We learn that holding ourselves small will keep us safe. We end up learning to be afraid of our strengths and our power – because they would force us out of our shrunken comfort zone and force us to face the as yet unknown aspects of our own capabilities.

Playing small serves no-one. It prevents us from living up to our true potential, it stops us contributing to those around us in ways that make a significant difference, and it sets an example for others that minimising ourselves is a valuable strategy.

Unless we take that step out of our comfort zone, how do we truly know what we are capable of?

Unless we put ourselves under the stress of uncertainty, how do we learn what we need to learn, and adapt in ways that make our comfort zone so much bigger?

The truth is that we were designed to shine. We were designed to take the leap and find out that what we are now is not the limit of what is possible. We are creatures of growth, adaptation and learning. By holding ourselves small, we hold ourselves powerless. We hold ourselves at the mercy of the opinions of others - which are of intense interest to them, but should only be curiosities for us.

And as we shine, and step into our bigger games, we role model and encourage others to step up into their better versions of themselves. By always being the one who goes first, we make it safe for others to explore their potential and possibility.

This is not about blind risk taking, but rather accepting that you are more than you believe. By truly accepting that one fact - and not being afraid of the true power that you can be (and have) - the comfort zone becomes a kernel of something that can expand and grow. As your comfort zone expands with your growth, what was difficult becomes easy. What was scary becomes comfortable.

As you shine, you create the space for others to shine along too. As everyone steps up and creates from possibility rather than fear, imagine what can truly be achieved?

Do not fear what you may be capable of. Instead, go out and find it.

Responsibility - Find out what you are truly responsible for.

There is a misconception that 'responsibility' is about carrying the weight of the world on your shoulders. This misconception extends to believing that we have to be perfect, that we will let ourselves and others down if we don't meet some crazy, misguided benchmark. It also extends to how we believe we need to compare ourselves to others.
In truth, you are 'responsible' for none of these.

If we break the word down we unlock a different meaning.

Responsibility = Response + Ability

Therefore the only thing you are truly responsible for is your ability to respond.

In life, you will be faced with a range of circumstances beyond your control. Good things and bad things can happen, regardless of what you have done. You are not responsible for what other people do, say or feel. You also have no control over things which happen randomly.

Unless you have a time machine or a super power, you also have no capability to control the future or the past.

So if all of these are true, then the only thing you can be responsible for is how you choose to respond to these external, even random circumstances.

In your life, understanding that it is not what happens, but how you choose to respond, is the key to creating a valuable experience. In every moment, your choice of response is entirely yours. You can respond emotionally, you can respond out of fear, or you could even respond out of your best version of you. This means that you can choose to respond to your circumstances by asking great questions, choosing great actions that take you forward toward high value outcomes, and from your strengths.

Sometimes, in some circumstances, the best you can do is simply the best that you can do. Sometimes coping and surviving is the best that you can achieve. Vicktor Frankl survived a concentration camp by realising that his life had extraordinary meaning beyond that experience. His being in that camp was beyond his control, but by acting in every moment in ways that got him through, he survived where others gave in to their circumstance and perished.

May it be true that you never experience this type of circumstance. However, it demonstrates that your responsibility is only choosing the best quality action to take you forward, regardless of the circumstance that you may find yourselves in.

As you create the experience of your life, remain responsible. Choose the best response that you can and keep expanding your capabilities.

Find what makes you happy - The experience of life should be filled with happiness. However, often people look for happiness in the wrong place. Happiness is simply doing what you love, and being in the moment to enjoy it.

Happiness occurs when we are present. This means that we have to be paying attention to what is occurring around us, rather than being distracted by other things, such as the future (especially if we spend our time worrying about stuff), the past (remembering how things used to be, and comparing this experience to those), or living in other people's heads (spending our time wondering how other people will think or feel by what is going on). When we are drawn away from being present, we cannot create happiness.

In every magic moment (when we are both present and able to appreciate something positive about the experience) we have the possibility of creating valuable memories. When we are not really 'there', we are dissociated from our experience and have nothing positive to remember.

If you think about it, if you try to remember all of the things you worried about in the last 12 months, you will probably struggle to come up with a list. I imagine that when I am old, I will not enjoy looking back on everything I worried about, or what other people thought, but rather at those magic moments when I experienced the world around me, the people I love, and things that matter.

Create magic moments. Do what you love and be present to enjoy it. Be open to magic moments occurring where you least expect them, and be open to immersing yourself in the moments of life as they happen to you.

Believe in something - One of the crushing experiences of modern life is apathy. It is an insidious defence - whilst not caring means we cannot get hurt, it also means that we cannot deeply connect.

We learn that caring can be painful. Especially where our caring is used against us, or where we see people being frustrated or hurt by what they care about, apathy seems like a reasonable course of action.

However, apathy leads to disconnection, isolation, and minimisation.

Believe in something. Be passionate about something in your life. Everyone has to find their own 'thing', their own purpose; their special experience that they deeply care about.

By believing and inviting passion we start to connect and to care. It might feel a little risky, but caring leads to connection - to the thing you are passionate about, to others in your 'tribe' (who are passionate about the same things) and, importantly, to the better version of yourself.

It is up to you what you believe in. It is for no one else to say what has to be important to you. Whatever you choose, choose it because it is something you believe in and are passionate about - not because other people are passionate about it.

Love the dog. Often people believe that their dog 'loves' them. In truth, it is not possible to know. We have trained the dog to be attached to us, and it has trained us to pet it, feed it and care for it in ways that are to its benefit. Pet owners get so much out of their pets, not because their pet 'loves' them, but because of the love they express for the dog. It really is a case that caring deeply is what is incredibly rewarding. It is the act of giving love and care, rather than receiving it, that makes our world a better place.

When you care - when you break out of 'apathy' - the world takes on meaning. You discover a purpose. You start to create experiences, magic moments, and a fulfilling life. In the end, that is all I could ever hope for you. So live beyond tolerance, shine, take responsibility, find what makes you happy, and believe and care. The rest is window dressing on the life that this will create.

Better world

We live in a world where it is easy to say 'what I do does not matter'. However, it is often the smallest pebble that can start a landslide. Whilst we may struggle to believe that we can impact at a global scale, we can make a massive local impact, and due to the interconnectedness, the reciprocity function, the nature of resource and the indomitable human spirit - the world really is ours to change.

If we are apathetic - and leave the destiny of the world to others - can we expect anything other than the lowest common denominator and self-interest to emerge? However, there are deeper truths about our place in this world that should make us acutely aware that apathy is not a functional solution - our world needs us all to act in bigger ways to create a world that we can be proud to leave to those who follow.

Interconnectedness - You may have heard of the butterfly effect - a butterfly flaps its wings on one side of the world, and this leads to changes in weather on the other. We know from natural systems that symbiosis and interconnectedness are the norm, not rare events. Whole forests have been shown to be interconnected by underground fungi. We know that ecosystems are so finely balanced that every insect, species of grass and animal has a role and a place.

Humans are interconnected, too. The actions that we take have repercussions in ways we cannot imagine. Often it is too easy to go through life seeing yourself as just an individual amongst the masses. The small choices you make only believing to affect you. And yet, through interconnectedness, even your smallest actions matter.

You get the choice to view yourself as part of something bigger - part of a family, a local community, a global collective. If you take this stance it encourages you to consider every action and weigh its impact. It is not about you, it is about you and so much more. When we act from our best - and most aware - self, you can enjoy the sense of connection. You can seek out those that you are connected to and revel in the sense of belonging. You can take responsibility for your every action, knowing that they all extend beyond you.

Reciprocity - Robert Cialdini introduced the concept of reciprocity as a means of influence. Our interconnectedness ensures that we are always having an impact on others and the 'law of reciprocity' suggests that when we give someone something, regardless of how small, it constructs social pressure for a reciprocal action to come back to us, as a way to 'balance the ledger':

- If you do something nice for someone, you are encouraging them to do something nice for you;

- If you do something bad to someone, you encourage them to return it in kind;

- If you give nothing and only take, you are encouraging others to stop giving to you, and teaching them to find ways to take.

When you hold yourself back you encourage others to hold back from you. The true joy of life (for us and for others) is in those small moments that matter. We can either go first, or hold back and wait for someone else to go first. Imagine the two different worlds this creates:

- A world where everybody holds back. Where we wait for others to lead us, to support us, to motivate and encourage us;

- A world where we step up. Where we decide to go first – to give, to lead, to set a standard for others. To give to create – and sharing in the joy that this value creates.

The way to make a difference is to simply go first. Do nice things, not because you have to, but because you like to. The greater the giving, the greater the getting back.

Remember, what you get back may not be what you expect. That is the joy of the uncertainty of life – imagine if you were everything you could be, what that would create for others, and therefore for you?

The world we live in is one truly built on interconnectedness, reciprocity and collaboration.

Enough - Humans have evolved systems that encourage us to forget what 'enough' looks like. We started with a concept that we could trade. We would trade excess of what we had, for something that we wanted or needed. Perhaps people exchanged excess chickens for much needed vegetables, or tools for fabric. We then invented money, and we were able to hoard this excess. This became a way of keeping score. Unfortunately, as people got a sense that they had to 'win', and what they possessed mattered, they lost sight of the idea of 'enough'.

There is an amount that represents 'enough' - enough to eat; enough shelter; enough in reserves. The rest - that is just for keeping score.

What if it was OK to know what 'enough' was for you? What if you didn't have to rate yourself on what you had, but rather on what you *did.* Knowing that small things can make a big difference to people that don't have enough, imagine if you could *do* something for them that changed their lives in ways you couldn't even begin to imagine, but which still left you with enough?

We each contribute to the world in which we live. I would encourage you to see yourself as part of a bigger world that you can influence through every small action that you take. Be optimistic – see that there is so much potential for good, for kindness, and creating a legacy of which you – and your generation – can be proud.

Be a shareholder of the community

Based in the USA, Russ is:

- Founder of Oliver Russell – who provide brand-marketing services to purpose-driven companies from the Fortune 500 to social entrepreneurs
- A member of the B-Corp global movement of business leaders seeking to redefine success, so that companies compete not only to be the best in the world, but to be the best for the world
- Has started four companies and five non-profits
- Winner of the American Advertising Federation's Silver Medal Award for outstanding contributions to advertising

Here is the advice he would give to his grandchildren...

Better business

In matters of your professional life, always strive to follow the light. Seek work environments where people possess positive energy, where possibility is prized over improbability, and business seeks outcomes that create social and environmental impact alongside bottom-line profit.

Better life

Be generous.

With others, be generous. Give freely of your time, your spirit, and your resources, whatever they may be.

With yourself, be generous as well. Life will be hard enough on you. And if you're anything like me, you'll be even harder on yourself, to the point of damaging your potential in this world. So be generous with yourself. Not in a selfish sense or as a false escape from the reality of commitments, expectations, and performance. But with a generosity of spirit that allows you to find peace with your imperfections, the missed opportunities, and the multitude of mistakes you will make throughout your life.

Better world

Don't view 'giving' as a philanthropic exercise of writing cheques to non-profits and other worthy causes. Be active and engaged in your giving. Volunteer! Get your hands dirty. Build sweat equity as a shareholder of your community. Don't limit your service to causes with which you are comfortable - push your boundaries with work that benefits underserved populations: the poor, the marginalized, the tragically unfortunate.

And if you are able, volunteer in lands far distant from your home, foreign to your understanding. This bit of magic will collapse time and space and make your world both bigger and smaller at the same time. No small trick, providing a gift and a source of energy from which you will draw upon for the rest of your life.

Respect everyone, experience everything

Based in Australia, and having worked in the UK and USA, Sally:

- Is passionate about helping accounting firms and small businesses embrace cloud accounting technology
- Has over 15 years of experience working in the software and accounting industries
- Played a pivotal role in launching Xero in Australia and contributing to its growth and success – and is now focussed on both the customer and partner experience, making sure they are the heart of the business
- Uses social media very actively to talk about social selling and accounting industry trends

Here is the advice she would give to her grandchildren...

Better business

Firstly, never lose sight of your customer. Your customer is everything, don't ever keep them waiting and don't ever stop listening to them. They are the reason businesses are successful and play a huge part in making sure you are always doing the right thing.

For every decision you need to make, look at your business through your customer's eyes. Thank, celebrate and support your customers, they have supported you on the journey and are part of your community.

Secondly, always hire smarter than you. This is a piece of advice I am going to borrow from someone who has been very supportive of my career, and continued to push me outside of my comfort zone. Doing this, hiring the right people, and surrounding yourself with people who are much smarter than you are, is a key contributor to your success.

Always hire someone who can take over from you and make sure you are always doing yourself out of a job.

Better life

Treat everyone the way you wish to be treated, with respect. It is the little things in life that make a difference to people's day, and how they feel. So always be kind and smile as much as possible. And remember, it is just as rewarding for you as it is for them when you make someone's day.

Better world

Above all try to experience as much of the world as possible. Seize every opportunity to travel. The world is fascinating. And to see and experience the many cultures, food, people and landscapes of the world is life changing.

So don't let fear or time get in your way. Not only will you experience all the world has to offer, but travel will grow your network of friends, family and memories.

Travel will also give you a much better appreciation of the world, and your place it in. It will help you understand how lucky you are. And it will help you to see what you can do to help those who are less lucky.

Travel will be a blessing and a joy. It will make your world better. And it will help you to make the world better for others too.

Give more, receive more, share more

Based in Australia, Sarah:

- Teaches business owners and leaders how to take care of their personal energy so they never burn out
- Co-founded the Gamechangers GO programme to stimulate people to lead with wisdom, purpose and integrity.
- Trained for 22 years with Chinese Energy Masters.
- Has worked with leaders and teams in global organisations such as Virgin Media, Bank of America, Dow Jones as well as many small and medium sized businesses.
- Is the author of the books 'Energy On Demand: master your personal energy and never burn out' and 'Love Money, Money Loves You'.

Here is the advice she would give to her grandchildren…

Better business

If you go into business, or even work for someone else, you will have to clarify your relationship with money at some point.

Your forefathers have had some very strange feelings about money. Some of them were embarrassed about it or never spoke about it at all, as if it were something shameful that needed to be kept hidden from public eye. Others saw it as their saviour and chased it all their life in the hope that once they had enough of it they would find happiness. Some enjoyed it and some hated it. Some had a lot of it and some had very little indeed. Some invested it and some gave it away. Some shared it and some hoarded it. These were all common attitudes towards money in the 20th and early 21st centuries.

The problem is that whether they wanted it or shunned it, their confusion about money led them to work in ways that created great damage. It was common for people to work so hard to make money that they actually damaged their health and wellbeing in the process. It seems extraordinary that they couldn't see this for themselves, but it was like a fashion - something that everyone did without thinking it through personally. They never realised that working hard is not the key to money. They'd been educated that way and they rarely questioned it.

Some of them led businesses that created damage to their environment. They used materials that ended up hurting animals or depleting the land. They made products they wouldn't give to their own families for fear they might be unsafe. They promoted foods, drinks, activities and entertainment that they knew were hurting the people who bought them and they didn't seem to care. There were many hair-raising stories that seem barbaric in hindsight. They took it as normal because they were afraid of money.

Some of them became very wealthy. They possessed the vast majority of the money that was flowing around the planet at that time. They could do whatever they wanted because they had unlocked some of the secrets of money and they knew how to create more of it in their lives. But there was one very strange thing - many of the people on the planet were living in great poverty at the same time. They didn't know how to create any wealth whatsoever. Some of them didn't have enough to feed their own children or send them to school. Everyone knew this and some people tried very hard to change it. But it wasn't as easy as it should have been.

There was enough money for everyone, especially because some people knew how to create more of it, but no one seemed to notice this. Many very wealthy people were afraid of losing their money, so they didn't share their expertise with others. Many poorer people were angry that they had less, so they didn't want to learn the secrets of the rich. They felt money was evil, even though they still wanted a lot more of it than they had. It's hardly surprising that everyone was so confused.

Looking back on it, there's one thing all those people had in common, regardless of how much or how little money they had. They were afraid.

They were afraid of not having enough, not being able to pay their bills, losing what they had, being in debt, having too much, being greedy, being poor, being immoral, being manipulative, being ordinary, being weak, being powerless, being powerful. They were afraid of everything to do with money. They didn't understand what money is and they treated it like some pieces of gold and silver that someone else can steal when you're not looking. This was very primitive.

They didn't understand that money, in its essence, is an energy. It's a vast system that allows us to create and share the products of our talents and gifts around the world. It facilitates the flow of human giving or generosity.

Anyone who is willing to give some of their service to others, in whatever form, participates in this energy. Whether it is rewarded in cash or some quite different form, the moment you give to another person you create a shift of energy, which means your gift will be returned to you many times over.

This is not something you can see or feel. But you will experience it if you approach money with a new relationship.

My advice to you is to love money. Cultivate a relationship of genuine love towards this energy that will serve you with great abundance if you allow it. Explore with your heart what it means to love and what it means to love money.

Love is never greedy or afraid. It's endless and expansive and has no need to score points or outdo another person. Love creates and shares freely, knowing there is always more to come. It heals whoever it touches and sees the beauty in life, even where there is suffering and hardship.

If you approach money with love you will always want to give more. This is not giving away your hard-earned cash to prove yourself worthy, but creating wealth through enjoyment and generosity, and then sharing it naturally because you can. Why would you do otherwise?

But I have one warning. This is a big change. It's easy for us to laugh at the primitive ways of your predecessors. But those ways are etched into your DNA, and it's your job to change them. You too may experience fears. You will know them because they will make you feel uncomfortable or unhappy. If you ever experience a negative feeling towards money you can be sure it's based in fear.

The opportunity you have is to switch to love. Open your heart and love money, and see how your life changes. Be kind towards yourself and others, especially in their fearfulness, and persistent in your quest to love money.

The more you love money the more your business will become a pleasure. You will no longer do those crazy things we used to do in the name of money - ignoring our own and others' wellbeing. You will create benefit for others and be rewarded for it. The more you give the more you will receive. The more you receive the more you have to share.

You will be creating and contributing to the economy through your love of money. This is a service to all of us, rich and poor. A genuine love of money creates great business. And great business creates wealth for all, not just for the few.

Earn with love, pay with love.

Better life

My advice here is to show up fully. Even though, from day one you'll be encouraged not to show up fully.

When you're a tiny baby you'll be taken out to be viewed by friends of your parents. If you smile and gurgle in a nice way everyone will be so pleased. If you scream, perhaps because you're having a bad day, it will have to be explained away. They will be relieved when you start to smile again. That makes you a good baby. You will have no idea at that time what's going on, but I'm sure you'll feel it.

Over the next seven years you'll be trained, day in day out, in what's expected of you. There will be behaviours that will get you labelled a good girl or boy. And there will be others which will make you naughty, disappointing, even unacceptable at times. It may be mystifying. One day you'll be sent to your room because you get angry and stamp your feet - your Mum will be screaming at you. It might be scary, and you won't have time to figure out why she's allowed to be angry but you aren't. It happens all the time.

At primary school you'll discover a whole new set of rules. Every teacher will be different. One of them will like it when you ask questions and another will tell you you're being noisy. One will be very easy going and another will be very strict. And you'll get very good at pleasing them most of the time – because it's more comfortable that way.

As a teenager the pressure will really mount. You'll have new training now - from your friends, social media and celebrities. It could be hugely challenging to work out how to fit in, how to look right, feel right, talk right, behave right, be seen with the right people, avoid the wrong people, be nice, be popular - and keep your family on your side. Sometimes it won't work at all and you'll feel like giving up. You may want to stay in bed and do nothing, so you don't have to face the world. You may even wish you could just stop, put everything on hold or start life all over again. Many of us have felt that at some time.

And it's going to continue for many more years. Pressure will come from every angle to tell you who you're supposed to be - at work, as a parent, in your community, as a partner, lover and friend, as a leader or follower - wherever you look you'll find people waiting to show you what's expected of you.

But the thing is it doesn't work that way.

People will put so much effort over the years into trying to control you, tame you, socialise you and make you acceptable. But inside you there's another person who can't ever be tamed, who doesn't want to be controlled, who is naturally social (and doesn't need so many rules) and is far more acceptable to others than the person they will try to turn you into.

Inside you is a person who came to this planet at this time, to be someone unique. I don't know who you will be, and maybe you're not so sure yet either, but there's no one else like you and there never will be. Sometimes it feels like a challenge to find that person, a kind of obstacle course or treasure hunt, where the winner finds herself and the losers try to be what someone else wants them to be.

So I want to give you a simple piece of advice to follow throughout your life, because this will help you find the treasure inside you.

Show up fully.

Whatever you're doing, show up fully.

That means put your heart into everything you do, do things well and make wise choices. It means respect yourself and your personal perspective on life (after all there's no one else like you) and share your life with others as fully as you can. It means connect with other people, see their uniqueness and show up for them as fully as you can too.

In the end it will mean whatever you want it to mean, but one thing is for sure. When you're showing up to please other people and fit in, you feel you're only half-alive. When you show up fully, you may still fit in and you may very well please others, at least some of the time, but you feel 100% present and alive.

Better world

It's easy to rant and rave about the state of the world. There's so much wrong with it, and anyone can see that. Just look at politics, or education, or health systems, or government, or business, or poverty, or the media, or families, or the elderly... and that's just the beginning.

But every minute you spend ranting and raving you are adding to the problems. You're spending time talking about them, giving energy to them, fuelling interest in them and stimulating others to do the same. In the end you contribute to the problems yourself, just when you wanted to change them.

This is one of the great contradictions of change. The more change is needed the more important it is not to give energy to what's wrong. Otherwise the change becomes even bigger and less likely to happen. You build a wall of resistance that needs to be overcome in addition to the change that is already needed.

So what can you do instead?

The simple answer is to try it out with yourself first.

It's easy to feel angry at people who are angry - terrorists, criminals, people who do crazy things.

It's easy to feel powerless in the face of people who are powerless - refugees, the poor, the sick, the victims.

It's easy to threaten people who threaten you - immigrants, authority figures, people with different beliefs.

And it's easy to justify your anger in the face of their (greater and less acceptable) anger; your powerlessness over their greater (and therefore insoluble) powerlessness; your (justified) threats over their (unjustifiable) threats.

But it's all the same behaviour. You are angry. They are angry. Anger is anger. There are degrees of it. But they are degrees of the same thing. And when has anger ever created a long-term solution to any problem?

You feel powerless at their powerlessness. You can't help if they can't help themselves. And if they *can* help themselves they don't need your help anyway. They've given up because it's all too hard. And you've given up because it's too hard for you to solve the problems. You have both given up. It's the same thing.

They threaten you. You threaten them. You feel justified in your threats - but so do they. You don't believe in their justification, but they don't believe in yours either. You feel morally superior because you can see what they're doing is wrong. And how do they see you?

What I discovered, much to my dismay at times, is that whenever I want to rant about someone else's behaviour I am the same as them. Not exactly the same, but enough for me to wonder what justification I have to be angry because my husband is angry; or to feel powerless to help someone in deep pain because they have so little power to help themselves; or to threaten someone who's threatening my security. We are all the same - just different degrees of the same colours and tones of humanity.

Sometimes we make grand plans to go out and change the world. That's great - the help is certainly needed. But again and again I find myself drawn back to reflect on myself. If I change the world and I'm fuelled by anger, what difference am I really going to make? To add some more anger to an already angry mess?

If I sit around and say I can't help, because I feel so powerless at the powerlessness of so many people, again what difference am I making? Adding more to an already overwhelming mass of disempowerment and weakness?

So when you hear yourself starting to rant about something that's going on in the world, even inside your own mind, stop for a moment and reflect. Do you want to add to the world's ranting? Isn't there enough of that already?

And ask yourself who you're choosing to be in this situation. Are you powerless or powerful? Are you angry or will you choose to find peace? Will you try to out threaten the threats, or will you find another level to negotiate?

Your response will depend on whether you're looking at the long-term or short-term. If you don't care about the future be angry, be powerless, make threats. You can sort the consequences out later. But don't be surprised if there's a bigger mess to deal with next time.

If you want to make the world a better place, make your choice wisely and be prepared to make it over and over again. If you want the world to be less angry, first try it out for yourself and see how it goes. It's not easy - especially when you feel justified in your anger. And if you want powerful solutions to the world's great problems, try being powerful yourself. That's going to keep you busy for many years.

For sure there'll be no more time for ranting.

Give, receive and nurture

Based in Indonesia:

- Dali and Finn Schonfelder founded the Nalu streetwear clothing brand in 2011 when they were only 11 and 8 respectively
- Their purpose is to break the poverty cycle in India by giving children the opportunity to stay on at school
- For every five products sold they give a school uniform to a child who would be forced to leave school without one
- To date over 7,500 Indian children have been helped to build better lives
- As inspiring young entrepreneurs, Dali and Finn are also asked to speak at conferences all over the world
- Vismai and Jyoti Schonfelder are their parents, and make it possible for their children to do all of this

Here is the advice they would give to their grandchildren...

Better business

Protect the goose (your business) that produces the golden eggs (your profit).

This is an accurate metaphor to help build long-term respect and commitment for your business. As your business evolves along a timeline - from infancy to adolescence, and finally into maturity - different care is required of it.

In the early years a lot of energy goes in, and often very little reward comes back. Chaos often signifies growth, as you struggle to develop your operations to cope with the new business coming in. As the owner it's important here to keep a helicopter view of where you want to take your business over the long term. Remove yourself from it at well-planned intervals so that you can work 'on' it, not necessarily 'in' it.

During the adolescence phase, your team will begin to function like a team rather than as a group of individuals. Invest in your team at this stage. Allow more time than anticipated to choose your staff and investigate the private values of potential employees - skills can be learnt but values are far too difficult to change, especially during adolescence. Go away together to industry seminars and get to know one another personally.

Take care of your team. Because your team is where you get traction.

Stephen Covey, in his book 'The Seven Habits of Highly Successful People', shared the concept of filling up the emotional bank account of your staff in good times in order to handle the inevitable difficult times with a sense of stability together. And he was so right.

Interestingly, the state of your business as it enters maturity is the product of how you have cared for it during the early years. It might seem counterintuitive, but we believe that there is very little that can be done to change the DNA of your business during the maturity stage. So if you took great care of the goose at the beginning, maturity is the time to reap your reward of golden eggs.

And we have noticed that golden eggs come in many different forms: time, money, health, peaceful mind, and an ideal work/life balance.

Better life

Life is precious. YOUR life is precious. ALL life is.

Every day is a gift, and every meeting with another person is a gift of this life to get to know yourself better, and to deepen this knowing.

Stay connected with your passion, with whatever makes your heart sing. Your passion is the core to your identity. Never forget to use your mind as a tool, as a servant and to keep your heart on the throne - your heart (which houses your passion) is the real king.

Business is not separate from life, and its success depends on finding a natural balance between receiving all that life offers you and giving back to life out of gratitude for what you have received. To be able to give, you first have to be able to receive fully, and to receive is to love yourself.

There is something called 'Entrepreneurial Passion'. Success is really passion translated into something tangible or real. Use all life's challenges to grow, learn and to get to know yourself - this is the ultimate goal of life, and business is just a really fun way of doing this!

Ask yourself: What was one challenge I had to overcome recently, and how did I use this as an opportunity to learn more about myself and grow stronger and more confident?

We would like to share a dream that one of us had recently:

'Once upon a time there was a princess and a prince, they were still young, however they knew they were destined to be lovers for life. She loved him dearly and could not imagine life without him. However one day the prince went into the forest to hunt and he got so lost that he couldn't find his way home anymore. After a long, long time wandering in the woods, he started to forget who he was. He couldn't remember that he was a precious son of the king and very, very rich.... an inner richness as well as outer wealth.

His princess saw what happened to him because she was so connected with her heart, and therefore with all of life around her, that she knew what was happening to her prince. The only thing she could do was to keep on loving him patiently until he would, one day, wake up out of this dream called life and find his way back home. Life would give our prince all the challenges and feedback to help him find his way home. This 'feedback' was sometimes beautiful when he would meet a gentle soul that would share their food with him. And sometimes not so pleasant... when he was cold and alone at night sleeping on the hard and cold ground.

One day, as he was wandering looking for some food and berries to eat, all of a sudden it felt like something struck him! He stood still and it was like time stood still too... he realised, he remembered WHO HE WAS! It felt like he was kissed from within by grace, it felt like he finally found home...

And the home he found was in his heart. He realised he had been carrying his home with him all along...

Once he realised his true nature, and feeling grateful and rich with all the life lessons he learned along the way, it was easy to find his earth home; the palace, his princess that had been waiting for him... needless to say they lived a very happy, wonder filled, life. And the scent of their hearts spread all over the country for more than 100 years...'

Better world

It is the true nature of all humans on our precious planet to receive and to give, and to have these two seemingly opposites balanced perfectly.

To be able to give, without depleting your energy source, you have to master the art of receiving. And that, our grandsons and granddaughters, is exactly what you as children are supposed to do! To receive... and that is actually all you are doing, because it is your very true nature to receive. As a young baby you cannot do anything else.

We remember when Dali and Finn were growing up. This receiving/giving dance flow seemed so effortless and natural. They would just as easily give something away that was no longer needed or wanted, or just simply because it is such a pleasure to make someone happy with a gift.

So you need to learn to take good care of you own needs and desires. You have to learn to take care of yourself first to be able to take care of others.

When the air pressure changes in the cabin of an airplane and the oxygen masks are released, you are encouraged to put your own mask on before you help someone else (eg your children). This is very important, because it has to do with self-love and self-care.

To give is so natural to our true nature, and to have a giving structure built into your life and business will support you more than you can imagine.

We have discovered that the balance between receiving and giving is essential. If you only give without receiving you will end up depleting yourself or your business (you'll end up having a burn-out). And if you receive without giving back, you'll hold on out of fear of not 'having enough', creating a stagnating life flow.

This is what we realised when we finally created a for-profit business where giving was a big part of its DNA. We noticed it 'flowed' more effortlessly than when we set up a charity. In contrast, with the charity it was sometimes difficult and frustrating raising funds and we felt the natural balance was lost.

Small businesses and family are the key

Based in Cambodia, Se is:

- Deputy director of the NGO This Life Cambodia, a sustainable community development initiative
- In that role he provides support for communities to develop the essential infrastructure, skills and programmes needed to make positive change in their lives and break free from poverty

Here is the advice he would give to his grandchildren...

Better business

Coming from a less developed nation and a community development background, I believe that every single human being, with no exceptions, should have access to the basic services that most of the world takes for granted, including education, healthcare, sanitation and diet.

I also believe that small businesses are one of the keys to making this happen, since by creating jobs, income and wealth they lift people, communities and countries out of poverty.

But so many young entrepreneurs in the developing world struggle to attract the funding they need to turn their small business ideas and dreams into reality. And so many struggle to get started.

So my advice is simple.

If you have more than enough money to live a comfortable life, don't waste the excess on frivolous spending. Instead, use it to invest in small business ideas in less developed nations. That way you will give the people there the opportunity to make things better. And you will also build an investment portfolio that is profoundly rewarding, both emotionally and financially.

And if you can't invest your money, invest your time instead. Connect with, advise and support young entrepreneurs. Help them find the funding they need. And encourage others to do the same.

Better life

Sadly, so much of the world is about ' I, me, my, mine...'.

But here in Cambodia we are very lucky because, in our culture, the focus is on family. And when I use the word 'family' I mean my wife, our six-month old daughter, my parents and my wife's parents, our brothers and sisters, our grandparents and everyone else in our extended family.

We are all very close, and always support each other. Family is a big part of our lives. We spend time together. We help each other. We talk. We share experiences. And we listen to each others' stories (even though we have heard some of them many times before).

We are also very proud of each other. And that is never more true than for parents and grandparents, who are always especially proud of their children and grandchildren. In fact, your parents and grandparents are never happier than when you are patiently listening to their stories and experiences, and of course, exchange yours with them.

It is also sadly true that nothing is permanent, and no one lives forever. Your family will not always be with you. So cherish the time you have together. Make the very most of it. And do it now, because you never know what tomorrow will bring.

The best way to live your life is to appreciate what you've got, be with the ones you love, and share your love with your family, your community and the world.

Better world

Unfortunately mankind has been ruining the planet, and continues to do so.

You already know why that has to stop, and why you must do what you can to make the world a better place.

So I'm not going to focus on the why. Instead I want to focus on the 'what' and 'how' that will help you to implement the business advice I gave to you above.

When you invest your time and money in small businesses in developing countries, make sure that the beneficiaries are going to use it wisely and that it will be used to make the world a better place. Personally, for example, I would make it a condition that they give some of their sales or profit to support a good cause in their community, ideally over the entire life of their business.

And when you are choosing a cause to support, make sure that the organisation behind it operates to the very highest standards. In particular check that they:

- Produce an annual report with an independent financial audit report – to ensure they are legitimate;

- Enforce a rigorous child protection policy – to ensure they make things better and not worse;

- Focus on making people feel happy - rather than making them feel guilty through 'miserable marketing' based on crying children etc;

- Have a plan to make themselves redundant – so that the underlying need for their support is addressed and removed; and

- Their work truly reflects and responds to the needs of individuals, families and the community – and is not in any way self-serving.

This is certainly not a definitive list, and I am sure you can add to it. But in my experience they really are vitally important considerations.

Ultimately of course, the way you choose to live your life is down to you.

But as your grandparent, I hope and pray that you will CHOOSE TO MAKE THE WORLD A BETTER PLACE!

Systematically do what feels right

Based in the UK, Steve is:

- Founder of the Accountants Changing the World movement
- Author of seven books, including 'The world's most inspiring accountants' and 'Stress proof your business and your life'
- A former UK Entrepreneur of The Year
- A Chartered accountant and founder of AVN, an association of over 100 proactive UK accountancy practices

Here is the advice he would give to his grandchildren...

Better business

My 30 years in business has taught me that there is a fundamental difference between having a job and owning a business: a job requires you to do the work personally, while a business does not.

However, the sad reality for many small business owners is that, in practice, they don't actually have a business, they have a job. Worse still, they are employed by a slave driver (themselves). And as a result they end up putting in more and more hours, and becoming more and more stressed.

But while the business owner keeps running out of hours in the day, their employees are often running out of things to do, because much of what needs doing 'can only be done by the owner'.

As a result, the lament "If only my employees could do things as well as I do, we wouldn't have a problem," can be heard through the clenched teeth of just about every business owner in the world. And that, my dear grandchild, is the lament that I want to help you avoid in your business.

Happily, the lament also contains the solution. All you need to do is turn it into the question: 'What do I need to do so that others in the business can do everything in the same way and to the same standard that I would do it myself?'

And then the answer becomes obvious.

You need to write down everything you do and exactly how you do it in the form of a set of detailed step by step instructions. These instructions then become the systems on which your business is based.

Your systems can take many forms (procedures manuals, written scripts, standard forms, checklists, software, cloud tools etc.) But once they have been created, they can be used to train and guide other people in the business to do the things that previously only you the business owner could do. So you no longer have to do any of those things personally. And you get your life back.

I have seen thousands of business owners benefit from exactly this approach. And I have also applied it in my own 25 person business with great effect (so much so that, at the age of 48, I was able to switch to a 90 day a year working arrangement).

Of course, I am not suggesting that systemising your business is an overnight job. For example, we have been systemising our business for over 15 years, and there is still more to be done. It is hard work, and it takes time. But, on a personal level alone, the rewards fully justify the effort, and are genuinely life changing.

You will be in control of your life. You will be able to choose how many hours to work, and how to spend those hours. And you will be able to spend more time on the other things that are important to you too, such as your family, health and hobbies.

As well as having personal benefits, systemising will also make your business much more successful:

- Systems allow you to step back from working IN the business and concentrate on working ON the business.

- The business is less dependent on any individual or group – because anyone can run the system. So you'll never need to fear staff illnesses, retirements, defections or industrial disputes again.

- The business is easier to grow - since its success can be replicated by others using the systems.

- The systems can be tested and improved in a systematic and scientific way. And, as a result, everyone ends up using the same optimal processes – rather than doing things in their own (often sub-optimal) way.

- What you do, how you do it and the results you get all become more consistent and predictable.

- So, for all these reasons, the business becomes more valuable and saleable – and probably more profitable too.

Better life

Whenever I have had to make a big decision in life, I have always let my heart act as my compass. And I urge you to do the same.

At university I was very good at economics, and had two degrees to prove it. What's more, I really wanted a career as an economist. But I also wanted to get married to your grandmother, Carol, and she had a job in Wakefield. It was a coal mining town 170 miles north of London, and there was certainly no chance of me being an economist there. So I had a difficult decision to make. But actually it wasn't a difficult decision at all. I simply let my heart be my compass. And as a result I moved to Wakefield, became an accountant instead of an economist, and Carol and I have been happily married ever since.

We have also had three wonderful children. But when our first child, Laura, was born I had another seemingly 'difficult' decision to make. My very well paid job as Head of Finance for the flagship £140 million division of a global blue-chip involved very long hours that meant I would hardly be around to see her grow up. So once again I used my heart as a compass, quit my job and spent the next six months as a very happy unemployed father, being there every minute of the day as Laura grew up.

Shortly afterwards I needed to make a third big decision: what was I going to do with the rest of my career?

I was offered a very good job - and a very big salary - at a household name company. It was certainly an attractive offer. But I knew I wanted to be around to see my children growing up. So, following my heart as my compass, I turned it down. And instead I set up my own business working from home in order to be there when my children came home from school desperately wanting to tell me about their day, and to be there at bath times and for bedtime stories. In fact, they still talk very fondly about how I read the first three Harry Potter books to them, all 2000 action-packed pages!

And on every level those three decisions turned out to be the best I've ever made.

As a husband and father I have a wonderful family and a joyful life. And my career ended up taking a path I could never have planned, giving me more pleasure than I could ever have imagined.

It worked for me. And I know it will work for you.

Better world

The key to making the world a better place is to combine my two previous pieces of advice... use your heart as your compass, and do so systematically.

Work out what feels right to you. What feels fair. What feels good.

And then create - or tap into - systems that help you to do what feels right, fair and good.

In my case that has included:

- Joining the B1G1: Business For Good movement – in order to surround myself with people who feel the same as I do;

- Using the B1G1 giving engine to automatically connect what my business does with causes that resonate with me – for example, for every one of my books sold we use B1G1 to give a child in Malawi clean water for life (and I specifically chose Malawi because of the profound effect the country had on my two daughters when they visited as school girls); and

- Setting up the Accountants Changing The World movement to encourage the accounting profession to make even more of a difference to businesses, communities, economies, the environment and the lives of people in need.

I have no doubt that you will find your own unique way of making a difference - driven by what feels right, fair and good to you, and supported by systems that make it happen.

And I have no doubt that you will make me a very proud grandfather – just as my children have already made me a very proud father.

Embrace change and engage with your values

Based in Singapore, Tim is:

- A global conference keynote speaker hired to motivate and inspire audiences of 10 to 10,000 people
- A trainer engaged by organisations, institutions, associations, churches and government ministries to motivate positive change, inspire action and create positive results
- Helps employees, managers, business leaders and business owners to become an even better version of themselves through his live and online training programs and solutions
- Multi award winning as both a speaker and business consultant
- Co-author of two books,
- 'Co-producer of Zoe, my amazing daughter, with my wife Lydia who is also amazing'

Here is the advice he would give to his grandchildren…

Better business

My first key piece of advice is… be coachable.

Being coachable means you can learn and implement advice, ideas and feedback offered by others. People who aren't coachable might still receive advice, ideas and feedback but instead choose to deflect, defend, doubt, delay, deliberate, destroy, devalue, demean, and ultimately do nothing differently. They may focus on making excuses, blaming others, blaming external circumstances, or criticising the feedback. The problem is that nothing changes. They don't change, they stay the same. If life is either growing or decaying, then businesses that grow do so because they change, and businesses that decay, do so because they refuse to adapt to the change around them.

It's the same with individuals in business. A person who seeks to grow, which inherently requires adapting and changing and learning new ways to do things even better, tends to be seen to be more of a team-player, more innovative and more willing and resourceful to deliver greater value to the team, their manager and their business. As a result they get promoted faster, earn pay increases faster, and generate greater profitability even faster too.

A study measuring 20,000 staff placements over a 3-year period asked managers why 9,800 of them failed - meaning they had either been fired, received a performance warning or received a negative performance review - within 18 months of being placed*. The study listed the top 5 reasons why people failed. The top 4 reasons were attitude-related and accounted for an enormous 81% of the failures! The fifth reason (11%) was that people didn't have the technical competence to do the job. The number one reason for failure as cited by managers was that the person was not coachable. Of the 9,800 people who failed, 26% were described as lacking the ability to accept and implement feedback from bosses, colleagues, customers and others. Their failure was because they were not coachable.

I have been that person in the past. While perhaps my intelligence, persistence, determination and stubbornness had often seen me succeed up to a level, there were times I couldn't progress because, once there, I wasn't coachable. As an employee I might have defended my perspective and felt like a victim as I was eventually let go. As a business owner I might have noticed a business decline or a plateau in growth. Upon reflection, these times seemed to have had a direct correlation to me not seeking, listening to or implementing the advice of trusted, aligned mentors. I needed to be more coachable.

It's foolish not to seek wisdom that can help for fear of looking weak. And it's the height of arrogance and the depth of delusion to think that you are the most skilled, intelligent, practiced and knowledgeable person in anything you seek to accomplish.

Surely if those who have walked the path before can share truths and illuminate a better way, and you can listen to and adopt their feedback, then your business life will see greater results, make a greater impact, deliver a better experience, create more joy, provide more positive challenges, and give a better life. So it is great that you are reading this and that you are interested in understanding the perspectives of others. The key to success will be your implementation.

---

*Details of this study by Leadership IQ can be found at
   http://wade.sg/hireforattitude

Here is what you can do right now: think of three people that you can ask to mentor you. Think of people whose values align with yours, whom you respect and are results-proven. One might be in your current business but outside your direct management hierarchy, like a more senior person in another department who might know of you. Another might be a trusted person in some other organisation or industry.

You could send them this: 'Hi [potential mentor's name], I'd like to ask your advice on a few challenges I'm facing. Because I respect your opinion and experience, I'd love to meet for an hour to discuss how you would suggest I move forward on these. Can I buy you lunch next Tuesday at 12:30pm at [place]? Thanks, [your name].'

Go ahead and email them right now to ask if you could connect with them. And if you can't afford to buy them lunch, meet them for coffee. If you can't afford that (I've been there), offer to meet them in their office.

Then listen, ask, listen and then – and here is the key piece of advice – ACT on the advice.

Be coachable. Receive feedback. Do something... worthwhile. Learn quickly. The fastest way is by doing. If it fails, you learn quickly. Possibly the stupidest way is to either risk everything or to risk nothing. Optimally, there will be some risk. And that risk means that failure is possible. This creates energy that you can translate into action.

If the meeting is useful, ask the person if they would agree to meet with you once a month for the next 4 months. If they do, great! You've established a regular mentoring session!

Oh, and if you'd like me to be one of the three, even if you aren't my grandchild, find me and connect. And if you're complaining that I'm not including my contact details here, then re-read this section. You're more resourceful than you think. There are also lots of people in this book that you might align better with. Seek and you shall find. And when you do, be coachable.

Better life

My advice here is equally straightforward... choose the right partner.

For me there are three relationship sets that matter most: the relationship I have with myself, the relationship I have with others, and the relationship I have with God. While in different circles I teach about all three, right now let's talk about your relationship with others. Specifically, let's talk about choosing the right partner.

Intimately, that will be your potential life partner. In business, that might be a business partner, a new staff member, a potential vendor or a customer, or a boss. Ultimately this will come down to seeking someone with an alignment of values, and their behaviours that demonstrate those values. Each of us can say we are committed to ideal values, but our decisions and behaviours will demonstrate our real values.

Choose the right spouse, business partner, mentor, staff member, vendor and customer by being able to invest time with them and understanding what their values might be, and which are most important to them. That investment, at the beginning, may save it from a messy ending. Choosing well at the beginning creates positive possibility. Choose poorly and everything can descend to darkness, bitterness, guilt, blame, destruction and hurt. Or you may simply waste a lot of time and resources. Choose well and you can create even more together with greater fulfilment, joy, and inner peace. You can create more value for each other, and those you serve.

Choosing the right partner creates a better life.

It may be easy to choose a partner based on convenient physical proximity, untested or uncontrolled chemistry, or temporal values. It may be easy, but they may not be the right partner. And be extremely wary of choosing someone if the majority of their conversation is about money.

The relationship I had before I met my wife was for a time thrilling, but then turned into the worst, most damaging relationship I have ever experienced. And the truth is, I knew she could be like that from the beginning. Don't ignore presently visible character weaknesses when making your decision. I did, and so did she to be fair. And it ended badly. While today I really hope she has transformed and found peace and love as I have, back then she had attempted to destroy and ruin me through character attacks and emotional terrorism. Yet for me the best part of that relationship was that, ironically, it was her who had dragged me back to church, and for *that* I will be forever grateful.

That's also where I eventually met my wife, Lydia. We were in a course together and happened to end up in the same discussion group. During the six months of that program, I was able to understand Lydia's values, fears, grief and joys. I could tell she had a caring heart from what she was sharing in the group, her interpretations of the course content, and her responses to others. And I value her desire to learn and grow and further develop, and that was evident in her simply being there.

What was unusual about that partner selection experience over any others was that this time I had six months to get to know Lydia and her values before we even got together. During that course we barely even had a one-to-one conversation outside of the group discussions. Only after the course did we start seeing each other, and 18 months later we were married. And it has been the best relationship I have ever had. I'm clearly blessed she married me. And now I really thank God for those six months too.

'Don't be unequally yoked,' a wise man called Paul once wrote to instruct a bunch of Corinthians about ensuring marriage partners had shared values and behaviours through beliefs. But values, behaviours and beliefs are not borne from the act of sitting in a religious building together or a membership to such an institution. Instead, they are borne in the heart of a person and demonstrated by their actions.

That's why evaluating shared values through behaviours and attitudes is valid for successful business partnerships too, because choosing a business partner can be similarly challenging. We could rush into partnership deals to eagerly advance the prospect of creating something amazing - only to later realise we're tied together in something structurally complex and our expectations and values are misaligned. Then the future of the relationship and the business is compromised and another mess is left.

While we're bound to make mistakes along the way - in choosing the right partner or in being the right partner for someone else - we can grow and learn from those mistakes to become the even better version of ourselves, making better decisions moving forward.

Past mistakes are not the disqualifier, only present character is. The wise writer I referred to earlier, Paul, also wrote of his hideous actions of the past when he was known as Saul. Paul's past didn't disqualify him only because he chose to transform his character and beliefs, to shift from destroying others to investing in the lives of others and to helping them grow.

I believe our lives are enriched, and can really be described as being better, when we are cultivating and sustaining better and deeper relationships, and when we are helping people grow. So invest more of your time and yourself into finding and nurturing the great relationships of your life. Invest in learning to select better. Invest in listening and asking questions, in being interested in understanding that person better.

What do they value? How are you aligned? How do you differ? Do your differences make you stronger together or are they deal-breakers? What are your shared goals? And then, importantly, what does the person decide to do, what do they actually do, and what do they say?

Invest well in choosing the right partner for both you and them. A considered choice is a heart-soul-mind-strength choice. It's a values-based choice, and that's based on what they value and how they are living their values.

And, from another of the three relationship sets that I think matter most, you can start by being more mindful and aware of how you're behaving, deciding, and what you're saying.

Better world

My third piece of advice is... to add significantly more positive value than you or your decisions consume.

The world must be more because you were here, not less. That might mean you are to teach a better way, to shape truths, to create solutions, to inspire action, to motivate positive change.

But the world is also inherently broken. It isn't a test of our character if everything is perfect. The storm makes the sailor. So if the world is broken, it means at times it isn't fair. Unfairness is a perceived violation of rules.

But we don't have to play the game with broken rules. Positive individual values remain and are evident everywhere. They are most commonly spelled out in positive religious or spiritual texts, encouraging love and growth, and a way, a truth and a life that is rightful living. They are evidenced in the way people choose to collaborate, to give, to help, to support, to honour and to love.

Yet the broken rules in the broken world pull us in another direction. Here people are encouraged to break the rules further, to compete, to take, to keep, to blame, to lie and to over-consume.

The world of consumption and excess tends to encourage people to violate their values in the pursuit of material wealth and media-framed images of what sellers want your definition of success to include. And it seems there is no real difference in the developed or the undeveloped economies in this. People seem to be taking advantage of people for their own gain. It's a short play and one bound to end badly, regardless of the outlier examples that tempt us to believe otherwise.

A better world comes from when we add significantly more positive value than you or your decisions consume. This doesn't mean a balance favouring your good deeds over your wicked ones. It means contributing more to this world than the world gifts you.

You have received so many gifts. You are given opportunities, given choices, given a chance, given feedback, given ideas. And you are given thanks, given service, given love, given an education, given an upbringing, given talents, given skills, given an environment, given a planet, and given... life.

And you consume it all.

And that's ok.

Because both parasites and blessings must consume it all to exist. But one leaves less and the other leaves more. Have you been a parasite or a blessing so far? We're all parasites for a time in our life. Some people just fail to metamorphose.

A better world is made when there is a greater increase in those who choose to be blessings. And to be a blessing means giving more gifts back so the world is better for us having been here.

Be a blessing. That's what you're here for. That's your purpose. To add significantly more positive value than you or your decisions consume.

Now work out how. Need help? Ask another blessing.

Be more self-aware

Based in Australia, Wayne:

- Is an expert in industry trends and how accountants can apply them in their practice
- Has over 30 years of experience working in the accounting industry
- Is an investor and Practice Advisor for Karbon
- Launched Xero in Australia, and was previously general manager for MYOB UK
- Has worked in Australia, China, UK and USA

Here is the advice he would give to his grandchildren...

Better business

Spend more time planning your future. Write down your 10 year, 5 year and 1 year goals, personal and business. It will be the best investment in yourself you'll ever make. Even if you don't achieve them, you're heading in the right direction.

Don't just let the future happen. You can control the direction - maybe not every step - but you're moving forward.

Don't sweat the small stuff. And take time to reflect on what you've achieved.

Be honest with yourself. Each year write down what you are good at, and what you know is never ever going to be your strength.

No seriously. Just because people expect you to manage staff and move up the corporate ladder, that does not necessarily reflect success or your ability. Never think that moving up the career ladder is the most logical step, as sideways steps can often lead to a better result.

This list will change over time and will allow you to plot where your next career and business step should take you.

You don't have to be an entrepreneur.

Just find your passion.

And recognize that your passion may change as your life changes, from being single to married, and perhaps even to having a mid-life crisis. It certainly has for me, since the passion I have now is so different to the country boy from Moama that just wanted a car.

Better life

Take that gap year and explore the world. You'll come back a better, wiser and more considerate person.

It's not about how many trinkets you collect in life. It's actually about giving more and expecting less. So don't be selfish.

Life is short.

You're counting down everyday. So any day above ground is a great day. And don't sweat the small stuff. Only people in the caring industry have a bad day - when sadly someone doesn't leave the operating table. For the rest of us, every day can be a great day.

Finally, everyone that I know who has retired seems to live a shorter life. So keep working - be it voluntary work or in advisory roles. And when you do, you will be more valuable than ever, because age gives you life experiences that cannot be taught.

Better world

Respect your partner, your children, your friends and people you don't know.

Be more tolerant of other people's points of view - and be entirely grateful that it's the simple lottery of life that has given you this opportunity.

Reduce your digital intake of information and increase your communication with others. The world is full of stimulating people when you give yourself a digital detox.

Leave a legacy – whether through the behaviour of your children, setting up a giving fund or incorporating a culture of giving in your business.

And most of all, give without expectation.

B1G1: The inspiration for this book

In June 2016 business leaders from across the world travelled to Bali. Technically it was to attend a conference. In reality, however, it was actually to celebrate a very special global movement.

Inspired by that movement, the delegates said 'let's write a book together'. And so this book was born.

That movement is www.b1g1.com, (also known as B1G1, Buy1Give1 and B1G1: Business For Good).

A message from B1G1's co-founder, Paul Dunn

'It's a delight to see this book 'make it'.

It was one of those 'out there' ideas that you sometimes hear - ideas that might just come to fruition if enough people really care.

And care they did! People who came to the first ever B1G1 Conference in Bali were seriously moved by the idea of collaborating to make something great and something that created a legacy.

Of course, in retrospect the B1G1 Conference was the perfect place to announce the idea. Because 'collaborating to make something great and something that created a legacy' is precisely what B1G1 is about.

To put it even more clearly, B1G1 is where giving, and hence caring, becomes business as usual.

By becoming part of this initiative, businesses of any size can make giving part of their everyday business and create a real impact on the lives of people around the world.

With almost 10 years of experience and nearly 100 million giving impacts, B1G1 is the leading online global platform for small-business giving.

B1G1 makes it easy for all companies (including yours) to support

amazing projects and then share that with your customers and
clients. And you get to join the international community of like-
minded businesses that really are changing our world.

Please visit **www.b1g1.com** to learn more about how your business
can do amazing things... just by doing what you normally do. It might
just be the most profound action you'll take in your life as a business
leader.'

If you too are inspired

By following Paul's advice and exploring **www.b1g1.com** you will find
the worthy causes that resonate most with you – and see the power of
small in action for yourself.

And if you want a recommendation, take a look at the worthy cause
'Free To Shine' – which helps prevent sex-trafficking in Cambodia. Five
of our authors are actively involved in it – one as the founder, one as the
managing director and three as Advisory Board members (including our
Dad). So it is very close to all of our hearts.

Other books written by the authors

The authors have written 38 other books that cover almost every aspect of building better businesses, better lives and a better world. In alphabetical order they include:

- *88 Essential secrets for achieving greater success at work* - Tim Wade
- *101 ways to make more profits* - Steve Pipe
- *Balance central* - Chris Wildeboer
- *Create the life journal* - Kerrie Phipps
- *Create your dream sanctuary* - Kerrie Phipps
- *Customer service* - Kerrie Phipps
- *DO talk to strangers: How to connect with anyone, anywhere* - Kerrie Phipps
- *Energy on demand: Master your personal energy and never burn out* - Sarah McCrum
- *Entrepreneur revolution* - Daniel Priestley
- *Giving business* - Masami Sato
- *How to build a better business and make more money* - Steve Pipe
- *I am woman* - Kerrie Phipps
- *Interviewing children: A guide for journalists* - Sarah McCrum
- *Intuitive* - Craigh Wilson
- *JOY: The gifts of acceptance, trust and love* - Masami Sato
- *Key person of influence* - Daniel Priestley
- *Lifting the lid on quiet achievers: Success stories of regional entrepreneurs* – Kerrie Phipps
- *Live your passion: People and performance* - Kerrie Phipps
- *Love money, money loves you* - Sarah McCrum
- *Mass participation sports events* - Chris Robb
- *Millionaire coach* - Heather Yelland
- *ONE: Sharing the joy of giving* - Masami Sato
- *Oversubscribed* - Daniel Priestley
- *Positive interactions: How to create memorable event experiences* - Kristy Castleton
- *Progressive practice: Disrupt yourself before others do* - Louisa Lee
- *Significance: How to align money and meaning in the well lived life* - Booth Aster
- *Social media secret sauce* - Adam Houlahan
- *Stress proof your business and your life* - Steve Pipe
- *Success 365: 365 great ideas for personal development and achieving greater success* - Tim Wade

- *The firm of the future* - Paul Dunn
- *The LinkedIn playbook* - Adam Houlahan
- *The solo travellers compass* - Kerrie Phipps
- *The UK's best accountancy practices* - Steve Pipe
- *The world's most inspiring accountants* - Steve Pipe
- *We are on the radio* - Sarah McCrum
- *Write right* (now re-released as *Write language*) - Paul Dunn
- *Your blueprint for a better accountancy practice* - Steve Pipe
- *Your blueprint for a better tax practice* - Steve Pipe

In some cases these books have been co-authored with others. However, for simplicity, the names of co-authors have not been included.

In addition, Dr Guy Campbell has been published widely in leading medical journals, including the following in 2015-16:

- *Rebate cuts will break Medicare*
- *If I ruled Medicare*
- *Care plans are an effective tool*
- *Guilty, I'm a GP who enjoys seeing drug reps*

About the editors

Based in Leeds, England, the editors are siblings who share much more than a surname. They all care deeply about the world, and are all determined to make a difference.

Jonathan Pipe

Jonathan has a degree in Mathematics, during which he spent a year living in Madrid becoming fluent in Spanish, teaching and embracing a new culture. He has a proven track record in leading, organising, and motivating people, and a passion for making things better. Having graduated in 2016 he is now determined to become a world-class business adviser.

His other main passion is music, where he has led three orchestras, performed internationally, won gold, silver and bronze medals in national and international singing competitions, and featured on Gareth Malone's BBC1 programme to find the UK's best singing group.

Katie Pipe

Katie graduated in late 2016 with a Masters degree in Marketing and Advertising. Her research into student engagement was published in a leading academic journal, and she used it to develop a new module which is now being taught to undergraduate students at Newcastle University, where she was also the elected President of a 200-strong student society.

Although her career in marketing is only just beginning, she has already helped a small professional services firm attract 58 people to their first ever seminar, converting 61% of them into customers, and generating 42 referrals. She also loves experiencing new cultures, and has travelled extensively in the Far East, India, Europe, Australasia, USA and Canada, and done voluntary work with children in Malawi.

Dr Laura Pipe

Laura studied Medicine at the University of Nottingham and is now a Junior Doctor. Having spent two years working in Yorkshire hospitals, she will start her training as a General Practitioner in 2017. Before that, however, she has taken a six month sabbatical to write this book and travel.

Beyond medicine, Laura's main interests are exploring new places, learning about different cultures and seeing local wildlife. She has volunteered with children in Malawi and Kenya, and spent time doing unpaid work in a hospital in Borneo. She also loves musical theatre, and spending time with her family, friends and fluffy ginger cat Charlie.

Contacting the editors

The editors can be contacted by email at **b1g1book@hotmail.com**

Appendix 4

Thanks and acknowledgements

Quite simply, this book would not have existed without the wonderful and inspiring contributions from our authors. Their open and honest insights, as well as their dedication and commitment to the project, have made our jobs as editors both enjoyable and extremely stimulating.

We are, as always, also hugely grateful to our wonderful parents, Carol and Steve Pipe, for their ongoing love, support and wisdom. Their continuing guidance throughout our lives, and their help and advice during the creation of this book, has been invaluable. We would like to thank them for this, and everything they do, with all our hearts.

Finally, we must extend enormous gratitude to the inspiration for this entire project... the B1G1: Business For Good movement, which continues to change businesses, lives and the world every single day.

Your advice to your grandchildren

This appendix contains a template and guidance which you can use to become one of the authors and create your own version of the book.

How to create your version of this book

Step 1 – Use the template below to capture the advice you would give to your own grandchildren.

Step 2 - Share your version of the book with your grandchildren, other loved ones, friends and anyone else you care about. You can also share it with your business prospects, contacts and customers.

Step 3 - Ensure that you follow your own advice.

How to get your version of the book printed

You can of course simply handwrite your advice on the pages that follow. Or even type it up on your computer, print it out, and staple/glue it in.

Alternatively, if you prefer, we can:

- Create a professionally produced version of the book for you that includes your content
- Supply it to you in both e-book format and as printer-ready artwork so you can have hardback copies printed
- Give you the right to distribute it in e-book or hardback formats to an unlimited number of people.

We will gladly do all of this for you because we want to maximise the book's impact across the world.

All we ask in return is that, in addition to reimbursing us for the small professional costs involved, you also make a giving via B1G1 for every copy you distribute. How much you give, and which of B1G1's hundreds of worthy causes you give to, is entirely up to you.

Please email us on b1g1book@hotmail.com for more information.

The template for creating your version

Use the blank pages that follow to answer these three questions:

Question 1 - If you could only pass on one piece of BUSINESS advice to your grandchildren, and you knew with absolute certainty that they would follow that advice throughout their time in business, what would that advice be?

Question 2 - If you could only pass on one piece of LIFE advice to your grandchildren, and you knew with absolute certainty that they would follow that advice throughout their lives, what would that advice be?

Question 3 - If you could only pass on one piece of advice to your grandchildren about MAKING THE WORLD A BETTER PLACE, and you knew with absolute certainty that they would follow that advice throughout their lives, what would that advice be? (NB: Your answer here might relate to the environment, philanthropy, peace or anything else. So please interpret and answer this question as you wish).

Printed in Australia
AUOC02n0819170217
283121AU00002B/2/P

2 370000 393364